BRITISH EN

ENGLISH
ITALIAN

THEME-BASED
DICTIONARY

Contains over 3000 commonly
used words

Theme-based dictionary British English-Italian - 3000 words
British English collection

By Andrey Taranov

T&P Books vocabularies are intended for helping you learn, memorize and review foreign words. The dictionary is divided into themes, covering all major spheres of everyday activities, business, science, culture, etc.

The process of learning words using T&P Books' theme-based dictionaries gives you the following advantages:

- Correctly grouped source information predetermines success at subsequent stages of word memorization
- Availability of words derived from the same root allowing memorization of word units (rather than separate words)
- Small units of words facilitate the process of establishing associative links needed for consolidation of vocabulary
- Level of language knowledge can be estimated by the number of learned words

T&P Books Publishing
www.tpbooks.com

ISBN: 978-1-78400-202-2

This book is also available in E-book formats.
Please visit www.tpbooks.com or the major online bookstores.

ITALIAN THEME-BASED DICTIONARY
British English collection

T&P Books vocabularies are intended to help you learn, memorize, and review foreign words. The vocabulary contains over 3000 commonly used words arranged thematically.

- Vocabulary contains the most commonly used words
- Recommended as an addition to any language course
- Meets the needs of beginners and advanced learners of foreign languages
- Convenient for daily use, revision sessions, and self-testing activities
- Allows you to assess your vocabulary

Special features of the vocabulary

- Words are organized according to their meaning, not alphabetically
- Words are presented in three columns to facilitate the reviewing and self-testing processes
- Words in groups are divided into small blocks to facilitate the learning process
- The vocabulary offers a convenient and simple transcription of each foreign word

The vocabulary has 101 topics including:

Basic Concepts, Numbers, Colors, Months, Seasons, Units of Measurement, Clothing & Accessories, Food & Nutrition, Restaurant, Family Members, Relatives, Character, Feelings, Emotions, Diseases, City, Town, Sightseeing, Shopping, Money, House, Home, Office, Working in the Office, Import & Export, Marketing, Job Search, Sports, Education, Computer, Internet, Tools, Nature, Countries, Nationalities and more ...

TABLE OF CONTENTS

PRONUNCIATION GUIDE

Letter	Italian example	T&P phonetics alphabet	English example

Vowels

Letter	Italian example	T&P phonetics alphabet	English example
A a	anno	[a]	shorter than in ask
E e	epoca	[e], [ɛ]	absent, pet
I i	vicino	[i]	shorter than in feet
i [1]	ieri	[j]	yes, New York
O o	ora	[o], [ɔ]	drop, baught
U u	uva	[u]	book
Y y	yacht	[j]	yes, New York

Consonants

Letter	Italian example	T&P phonetics alphabet	English example
B b	bambino	[b]	baby, book
c,cc [2]	città	[ʧ]	church, French
c,cc [3]	casa	[k]	clock, kiss
D d	donna	[d]	day, doctor
F f	frutto	[f]	face, food
g, gg [4]	giorno	[ʤ]	joke, general
g, gg [5]	grande	[g]	game, gold
H h	hotel	[h]	silent [h]
J j	jazz	[ʤ]	joke, general
K k	kiwi	[k]	clock, kiss
L l	latte	[l]	lace, people
M m	madre	[m]	magic, milk
N n	notte	[n]	name, normal
P p	parco	[p]	pencil, private
Q q	quadro	[k]	clock, kiss
R r	rosa	[r]	rolled [r]
s [6]	vaso	[z]	zebra, please
S s [7]	sbarra	[z]	zebra, please
S s [8]	testa	[s]	city, boss
T t	teatro	[t]	tourist, trip
V v	vita	[v]	very, river
W w	wisky	[w]	vase, winter
X x	fax	[ks]	box, taxi
Z z [9]	zio	[ʣ]	beads, kids
Z z [10]	bronzo	[ʣ]	beads, kids
Z z [11]	marzo	[ʦ]	cats, tsetse fly

Letter	Italian example	T&P phonetics alphabet	English example

Combinations of letters

Letter	Italian example	T&P phonetics alphabet	English example
ch	chitarra	[k]	clock, kiss
gh	ghiaccio	[g]	game, gold
gn	legno	[ɲ]	canyon, new
gli [12]	figlio	[ʎ]	daily, million
gli [13]	figli	[lji]	million, billiards
sc [14]	scienza	[ʃ]	machine, shark
sc [15]	scala	[sk]	risk, sky
sch	schermo	[sk]	risk, sky

Comments

[1] between vowels
[2] before
[3] elsewhere
[4] before e,i
[5] elsewhere
[6] between wovels
[7] before
[8] elsewhere
[9] at the beginning of words
[10] after
[11] after the other consonants
[12] at the beginning and inside
[13] at the end of words
[14] before e,i
[15] elsewhere

ABBREVIATIONS
used in the dictionary

ab.	-	about
adj	-	adjective
adv	-	adverb
anim.	-	animate
as adj	-	attributive noun used as adjective
e.g.	-	for example
etc.	-	et cetera
fam.	-	familiar
fem.	-	feminine
form.	-	formal
inanim.	-	inanimate
masc.	-	masculine
math	-	mathematics
mil.	-	military
n	-	noun
pl	-	plural
pron.	-	pronoun
sb	-	somebody
sing.	-	singular
sth	-	something
v aux	-	auxiliary verb
vi	-	intransitive verb
vi, vt	-	intransitive, transitive verb
vt	-	transitive verb

m	-	masculine noun
f	-	feminine noun
m pl	-	masculine plural
f pl	-	feminine plural
m, f	-	masculine, feminine
vr	-	reflexive verb

BASIC CONCEPTS

1. Pronouns

I, me	**io**	['io]
you	**tu**	['tu]
he	**lui**	['lyj]
she	**lei**	['lej]
we	**noi**	['nɔj]
you (to a group)	**voi**	['vɔj]
they	**loro, essi**	['lɔrɔ], ['ɛssi]

2. Greetings. Salutations

Hello! (fam.)	**Buongiorno!**	[buɔn'dʒɔrnɔ]
Hello! (form.)	**Salve!**	['saʎvɛ]
Good morning!	**Buongiorno!**	[buɔn'dʒɔrnɔ]
Good afternoon!	**Buon pomeriggio!**	[bu'ɔn pɔmɛ'ridʒɔ]
Good evening!	**Buonasera!**	[buɔna'sɛra]
to say hello	**salutare** (vt)	[saly'tarɛ]
Hi! (hello)	**Ciao! Salve!**	['tʃaɔ 'saʎvɛ]
greeting (n)	**saluto** (m)	[sa'lytɔ]
to greet (vt)	**salutare** (vt)	[saly'tarɛ]
How are you?	**Come va?**	['kɔmɛ 'va]
What's new?	**Che c'è di nuovo?**	[kɛ tʃe di nu'ɔvɔ]
Bye-Bye! Goodbye!	**Arrivederci!**	[arrivɛ'dɛrtʃi]
See you soon!	**A presto!**	[a 'prɛstɔ]
Farewell!	**Addio!**	[ad'diɔ]
to say goodbye	**congedarsi** (vr)	[kɔndʒe'darsi]
Cheers!	**Ciao!**	['tʃaɔ]
Thank you! Cheers!	**Grazie!**	['gratsiɛ]
Thank you very much!	**Grazie mille!**	['gratsiɛ mille]
My pleasure!	**Prego**	['prɛgɔ]
Don't mention it!	**Non c'è di che!**	[nɔn tʃɛ di'kɛ]
It was nothing	**Di niente**	[di 'njentɛ]
Excuse me! (fam.)	**Scusa!**	['skuza]
Excuse me! (form.)	**Scusi!**	['skuzi]
to excuse (forgive)	**scusare** (vt)	[sku'zarɛ]
to apologize (vi)	**scusarsi** (vr)	[sku'zarsi]
My apologies	**Chiedo scusa**	['kjedɔ 'skuza]
I'm sorry!	**Mi perdoni!**	[mi pɛr'dɔni]

to forgive (vt)	perdonare (vt)	[pɛrdɔ'narɛ]
It's okay!	Non fa niente	[nɔn fa ni'ɛntɛ]
please (adv)	per favore	[pɛr fa'vɔrɛ]

Don't forget!	Non dimentichi!	[nɔn di'mɛntiki]
Certainly!	Certamente!	[tʃerta'mɛntɛ]
Of course not!	Certamente no!	[tʃerta'mɛntɛ nɔ]
Okay! (I agree)	D'accordo!	[dak'kɔrdɔ]
That's enough!	Basta!	['basta]

3. Questions

Who?	Chi?	[ki]
What?	Che cosa?	[kɛ 'kɔza]
Where? (at, in)	Dove?	['dɔvɛ]
Where (to)?	Dove?	['dɔvɛ]
Where ... from?	Di dove?, Da dove?	[di 'dɔvɛ da 'dɔvɛ]
When?	Quando?	[ku'andɔ]
Why? (aim)	Perché?	[pɛr'kɛ]
Why? (reason)	Perché?	[pɛr'kɛ]

What for?	Per che cosa?	[pɛr kɛ 'kɔza]
How? (in what way)	Come?	['kɔmɛ]
What? (which?)	Che?	[kɛ]
Which?	Quale?	[ku'ale]

To whom?	A chi?	[a 'ki]
About whom?	Di chi?	[di 'ki]
About what?	Di che cosa?	[di kɛ 'kɔza]
With whom?	Con chi?	[kɔn 'ki]

How many?	Quanti?	[ku'anti]
How much?	Quanto?	[ku'antɔ]
Whose?	Di chi?	[di 'ki]

4. Prepositions

with (accompanied by)	con	[kɔn]
without	senza	['sɛntsa]
to (indicating direction)	a	[a]
about (talking ~ ...)	di	[di]
before (in time)	prima di ...	['prima di]
in front of ...	di fronte a ...	[di 'frɔntɛ a]

under (beneath, below)	sotto	['sɔttɔ]
above (over)	sopra	['sɔpra]
on (atop)	su	[su]
from (off, out of)	da, di	[da], [di]
of (made from)	di	[di]

| in (e.g. ~ ten minutes) | fra ... | [fra] |
| over (across the top of) | attraverso | [attra'vɛrsɔ] |

5. Function words. Adverbs. Part 1

Where? (at, in)	Dove?	['dɔvɛ]
here (adv)	qui	[ku'i]
there (adv)	lì	[li]
somewhere (to be)	da qualche parte	[da ku'aʎkɛ 'partɛ]
nowhere (not anywhere)	da nessuna parte	[da nɛs'suna 'partɛ]
by (near, beside)	vicino a …	[wi'ʧinɔ a]
by the window	vicino alla finestra	[wi'ʧinɔ 'aʎa fi'nɛstra]
Where (to)?	Dove?	['dɔvɛ]
here (e.g. come ~!)	di qui	[di ku'i]
there (e.g. to go ~)	ci	[ʧi]
from here (adv)	da qui	[da ku'i]
from there (adv)	da lì	[da 'li]
close (adv)	vicino, accanto	[wi'ʧinɔ], [a'kantɔ]
far (adv)	lontano	[lɔn'tanɔ]
near (e.g. ~ Paris)	vicino a …	[wi'ʧinɔ a]
nearby (adv)	vicino	[wi'ʧinɔ]
not far (adv)	non lontano	[nɔn lɔn'tanɔ]
left (adj)	sinistro	[si'nistrɔ]
on the left	a sinistra	[a si'nistra]
to the left	a sinistra	[a si'nistra]
right (adj)	destro	['dɛstrɔ]
on the right	a destra	[a 'dɛstra]
to the right	a destra	[a 'dɛstra]
in front (adv)	davanti	[da'vanti]
front (as adj)	anteriore	[antɛri'ɔrɛ]
ahead (in space)	avanti	[a'vanti]
behind (adv)	dietro	['djetrɔ]
from behind	da dietro	[da 'djetrɔ]
back (towards the rear)	indietro	[in'djetrɔ]
middle	mezzo (m), centro (m)	['mɛʣɔ], ['ʧentrɔ]
in the middle	in mezzo, al centro	[in 'mɛʣɔ], [aʎ 'ʧentrɔ]
at the side	di fianco	[di 'fjaŋkɔ]
everywhere (adv)	dappertutto	[dappɛr'tuttɔ]
around (in all directions)	attorno	[at'tɔrnɔ]
from inside	da dentro	[da 'dɛntrɔ]
somewhere (to go)	da qualche parte	[da ku'aʎkɛ 'partɛ]
straight (directly)	dritto	['drittɔ]
back (e.g. come ~)	indietro	[in'djetrɔ]
from anywhere	da qualsiasi parte	[da kuaʎsia'zi 'partɛ]
from somewhere	da qualche posto	[da ku'aʎkɛ 'pɔstɔ]

firstly (adv)	in primo luogo	[in 'primo ly'ɔgɔ]
secondly (adv)	in secondo luogo	[in sɛ'kɔndɔ ly'ɔgɔ]
thirdly (adv)	in terzo luogo	[in 'tɛrtsɔ ly'ɔgɔ]
suddenly (adv)	all'improvviso	[allimprɔv'wizɔ]
at first (adv)	all'inizio	[alli'nitsiɔ]
for the first time	per la prima volta	[pɛr ʎa 'prima 'vɔʎta]
long before ...	molto tempo prima di...	['mɔʎtɔ 'tɛmpɔ 'prima di]
anew (over again)	di nuovo	[di nu'ɔvɔ]
for good (adv)	per sempre	[pɛr 'sɛmprɛ]
never (adv)	mai	[maj]
again (adv)	ancora	[a'ŋkora]
now (adv)	adesso	[a'dɛssɔ]
often (adv)	spesso	['spɛssɔ]
then (adv)	allora	[al'lɔra]
urgently (quickly)	urgentemente	[urdʒentɛ'mɛntɛ]
usually (adv)	di solito	[di 'sɔlitɔ]
by the way, ...	a proposito, ...	[a prɔ'pozitɔ]
possible (that is ~)	è possibile	[ɛ pɔ'sibilɛ]
probably (adv)	probabilmente	[prɔbabiʎ'mentɛ]
maybe (adv)	forse	['fɔrsɛ]
besides ...	inoltre ...	[i'nɔʎtrɛ]
that's why ...	ecco perché ...	['ɛkkɔ pɛr'kɛ]
in spite of ...	nonostante	[nɔnɔs'tantɛ]
thanks to ...	grazie a ...	['gratsiɛ a]
what (pron.)	che cosa	[kɛ 'kɔza]
that	che	[kɛ]
something	qualcosa	[kuaʎ'kɔza]
anything (something)	qualcosa	[kuaʎ'kɔza]
nothing	niente	['njentɛ]
who (pron.)	chi	[ki]
someone	qualcuno	[kuaʎ'kunɔ]
somebody	qualcuno	[kuaʎ'kunɔ]
nobody	nessuno	[nɛs'sunɔ]
nowhere (a voyage to ~)	da nessuna parte	[da nɛs'suna 'partɛ]
nobody's	di nessuno	[di nɛs'sunɔ]
somebody's	di qualcuno	[di kuaʎ'kunɔ]
so (I'm ~ glad)	così	[kɔ'zi]
also (as well)	anche	['aŋkɛ]
too (as well)	anche, pure	['aŋkɛ], ['purɛ]

6. Function words. Adverbs. Part 2

Why?	Perché?	[pɛr'kɛ]
for some reason	per qualche ragione	[pɛr ku'aʎke ra'dʒɔnɛ]
because ...	perché ...	[pɛr'kɛ]
for some purpose	per qualche motivo	[pɛr ku'aʎke mɔ'tivɔ]
and	e	[ɛ]

or	o ...	[ɔ]
but	ma	[ma]
for (e.g. ~ me)	per	[pɛr]

too (excessively)	troppo	['trɔppɔ]
only (exclusively)	solo	['sɔlɔ]
exactly (adv)	esattamente	[ɛzatta'mentɛ]
about (more or less)	circa	['tʃirka]

approximately (adv)	approssimativamente	[aprɔsimativa'mentɛ]
approximate (adj)	approssimativo	[apprɔssima'tivɔ]
almost (adv)	quasi	[ku'azi]
the rest	resto (m)	['rɛstɔ]

each (adj)	ogni	['ɔɲʲi]
any (no matter which)	qualsiasi	[kuaʎ'siazi]
many (adv)	molti	['mɔʎti]
much (adv)	molto	['mɔʎtɔ]
many people	molta gente	['mɔʎta 'dʒɛntɛ]
all (everyone)	tutto, tutti	['tuttɔ], ['tutti]

in exchange for ...	in cambio di ...	[in 'kambʲɔ di]
in exchange (adv)	in cambio	[in 'kambʲɔ]
by hand (made)	a mano	[a 'manɔ]
hardly (negative opinion)	poco probabile	['pɔkɔ prɔ'babile]

probably (adv)	probabilmente	[prɔbabiʎ'mentɛ]
on purpose (adv)	apposta	[ap'pɔsta]
by accident (adv)	per caso	[pɛr 'kazɔ]

very (adv)	molto	['mɔʎtɔ]
for example (adv)	per esempio	[pɛr ɛ'zɛmpʲɔ]
between	fra	[fra]
among	fra	[fra]
so much (such a lot)	tanto	['tantɔ]
especially (adv)	soprattutto	[sopra'tuttɔ]

NUMBERS. MISCELLANEOUS

7. Cardinal numbers. Part 1

0 zero	**zero** (m)	['dzɛrɔ]
1 one	**uno**	['unɔ]
2 two	**due**	['duɛ]
3 three	**tre**	['trɛ]
4 four	**quattro**	[ku'attrɔ]
5 five	**cinque**	['ʧiŋkuɛ]
6 six	**sei**	['sɛj]
7 seven	**sette**	['sɛttɛ]
8 eight	**otto**	['ɔttɔ]
9 nine	**nove**	['nɔvɛ]
10 ten	**dieci**	['djeʧi]
11 eleven	**undici**	['undiʧi]
12 twelve	**dodici**	['dɔdiʧi]
13 thirteen	**tredici**	['trɛdiʧi]
14 fourteen	**quattordici**	[kuat'tɔrdiʧi]
15 fifteen	**quindici**	[ku'indiʧi]
16 sixteen	**sedici**	['sɛdiʧi]
17 seventeen	**diciassette**	[diʧas'sɛttɛ]
18 eighteen	**diciotto**	[di'ʧɔttɔ]
19 nineteen	**diciannove**	[diʧa'ŋɔvɛ]
20 twenty	**venti**	['vɛnti]
21 twenty-one	**ventuno**	[vɛn'tunɔ]
22 twenty-two	**ventidue**	[vɛnti'duɛ]
23 twenty-three	**ventitre**	[vɛntit'rɛ]
30 thirty	**trenta**	['trɛnta]
31 thirty-one	**trentuno**	[trɛn'tunɔ]
32 thirty-two	**trentadue**	[trɛnta'duɛ]
33 thirty-three	**trentatre**	[trɛntat'rɛ]
40 forty	**quaranta**	[kua'ranta]
41 forty-one	**quarantuno**	[kuaran'tunɔ]
42 forty-two	**quarantadue**	[kuaranta'duɛ]
43 forty-three	**quarantatre**	[kuarantat'rɛ]
50 fifty	**cinquanta**	[ʧiŋku'anta]
51 fifty-one	**cinquantuno**	[ʧiŋkuan'tunɔ]
52 fifty-two	**cinquantadue**	[ʧiŋkuanta'duɛ]
53 fifty-three	**cinquantatre**	[ʧiŋkuantat'rɛ]
60 sixty	**sessanta**	[sɛs'santa]
61 sixty-one	**sessantuno**	[sɛssan'tunɔ]

| 62 sixty-two | sessantadue | [sɛssanta'duɛ] |
| 63 sixty-three | sessantatre | [sɛssantat'rɛ] |

70 seventy	settanta	[sɛt'tanta]
71 seventy-one	settantuno	[sɛttan'tunɔ]
72 seventy-two	settantadue	[sɛttanta'duɛ]
73 seventy-three	settantatre	[sɛttantat'rɛ]

80 eighty	ottanta	[ɔt'tanta]
81 eighty-one	ottantuno	[ɔttan'tunɔ]
82 eighty-two	ottantadue	[ɔttanta'duɛ]
83 eighty-three	ottantatre	[ɔttantat'rɛ]

90 ninety	novanta	[nɔ'vanta]
91 ninety-one	novantuno	[nɔvan'tunɔ]
92 ninety-two	novantadue	[nɔvanta'duɛ]
93 ninety-three	novantatre	[nɔvantat'rɛ]

8. Cardinal numbers. Part 2

100 one hundred	cento	['tʃentɔ]
200 two hundred	duecento	[duɛ'tʃentɔ]
300 three hundred	trecento	[trɛ'tʃentɔ]
400 four hundred	quattrocento	[kuattrɔ'tʃentɔ]
500 five hundred	cinquecento	[tʃiŋkuɛ'tʃentɔ]

600 six hundred	seicento	[sɛj'tʃentɔ]
700 seven hundred	settecento	[sɛttɛ'tʃentɔ]
800 eight hundred	ottocento	[ɔttɔ'tʃentɔ]
900 nine hundred	novecento	[nɔvɛ'tʃentɔ]

1000 one thousand	mille	['mille]
2000 two thousand	duemila	[duɛ'miʎa]
3000 three thousand	tremila	[trɛ'miʎa]
10000 ten thousand	diecimila	[djetʃi'miʎa]
one hundred thousand	centomila	[tʃentɔ'miʎa]
million	milione (m)	[mi'ʎɔnɛ]
billion	miliardo (m)	[mili'ardɔ]

9. Ordinal numbers

first (adj)	primo	['primɔ]
second (adj)	secondo	[sɛ'kɔndɔ]
third (adj)	terzo	['tɛrtsɔ]
fourth (adj)	quarto	[ku'artɔ]
fifth (adj)	quinto	[ku'intɔ]

sixth (adj)	sesto	['sɛstɔ]
seventh (adj)	settimo	['sɛttimɔ]
eighth (adj)	ottavo	[ɔt'tavɔ]
ninth (adj)	nono	['nɔnɔ]
tenth (adj)	decimo	['dɛtʃimɔ]

COLORS. UNITS OF MEASUREMENT

10. Colours

colour	colore (m)	[ko'lɔrɛ]
shade (tint)	sfumatura (f)	[sfuma'tura]
hue	tono (m)	['tɔnɔ]
rainbow	arcobaleno (m)	[arkɔba'lenɔ]
white (adj)	bianco	['bjaŋkɔ]
black (adj)	nero	['nɛrɔ]
grey (adj)	grigio	['gridʒɔ]
green (adj)	verde	['vɛrdɛ]
yellow (adj)	giallo	['dʒallɔ]
red (adj)	rosso	['rɔssɔ]
blue (adj)	blu	['bly]
light blue (adj)	azzurro	[a'dzurrɔ]
pink (adj)	rosa	['rɔza]
orange (adj)	arancione	[aran'tʃɔnɛ]
violet (adj)	violetto	[wiɔ'lettɔ]
brown (adj)	marrone	[mar'rɔnɛ]
golden (adj)	d'oro	['dɔrɔ]
silvery (adj)	argenteo	[ar'dʒentɛɔ]
beige (adj)	beige	[bɛʒ]
cream (adj)	color crema	[kɔ'lɔr 'krɛma]
turquoise (adj)	turchese	[tur'kɛzɛ]
cherry red (adj)	rosso ciliegia (f)	['rɔssɔ tʃi'ʎjedʒa]
lilac (adj)	lilla	['liʎa]
crimson (adj)	rosso lampone	['rɔssɔ ʎam'pɔnɛ]
light (adj)	chiaro	['kjarɔ]
dark (adj)	scuro	['skurɔ]
bright (adj)	vivo, vivido	['wivɔ], ['wiwidɔ]
coloured (pencils)	colorato	[kɔlɔ'ratɔ]
colour (e.g. ~ film)	a colori	[a kɔ'lɔri]
black-and-white (adj)	bianco e nero	['bjaŋkɔ ɛ 'nɛrɔ]
plain (one colour)	in tinta unita	[in 'tinta u'nita]
multicoloured (adj)	multicolore	[muʎtikɔ'lɔrɛ]

11. Units of measurement

weight	peso (m)	['pɛzɔ]
length	lunghezza (f)	[ly'ŋɛtsa]

width	larghezza (f)	[ʎar'gɛtsa]
height	altezza (f)	[aʎ'tɛtsa]
depth	profondità (f)	[profondi'ta]
volume	volume (m)	[vo'lymɛ]
area	area (f)	['arɛa]

gram	grammo (m)	['grammɔ]
milligram	milligrammo (m)	[millig'rammɔ]
kilogram	chilogrammo (m)	[kilɜg'rammɔ]
ton	tonnellata (f)	[tɔŋɛ'ʎata]
pound	libbra (f)	['libbra]
ounce	oncia (f)	['ɔntʃa]

metre	metro (m)	['mɛtrɔ]
millimetre	millimetro (m)	[mil'limɛtrɔ]
centimetre	centimetro (m)	[tʃen'timɛtrɔ]
kilometre	chilometro (m)	[ki'lɜmɛtrɔ]
mile	miglio (m)	['miʎɔ]

inch	pollice (m)	['pollitʃe]
foot	piede (f)	['pjedɛ]
yard	iarda (f)	[jarda]

square metre	metro (m) quadro	['mɛtrɔ ku'adrɔ]
hectare	ettaro (m)	['ɛttarɔ]

litre	litro (m)	['litrɔ]
degree	grado (m)	['gradɔ]
volt	volt (m)	[voʎt]
ampere	ampere (m)	[am'pɛrɛ]
horsepower	cavallo vapore (m)	[ka'vallɔ va'pɔrɛ]

quantity	quantità (f)	[kuanti'ta]
a little bit of …	un po' di …	[un 'pɔ di]
half	metà (f)	[mɛ'ta]
dozen	dozzina (f)	[dɔ'dzina]
piece (item)	pezzo (m)	['pɛtsɔ]

size	dimensione (f)	[dimɛnsi'ɔnɛ]
scale (map ~)	scala (f)	['skaʎa]

minimum (adj)	minimo	['minimɔ]
the smallest (adj)	minore	[mi'nɔrɛ]
medium (adj)	medio	['mɛdiɔ]
maximum (adj)	massimo	['massimɔ]
the largest (adj)	maggiore	[ma'dʒɔrɛ]

12. Containers

jar (glass)	barattolo (m) di vetro	[ba'rattɔlɔ di 'vɛtrɔ]
tin, can	latta (f), lattina (f)	['ʎatta], [lat'tina]
bucket	secchio (m)	['sɛkkiɔ]
barrel	barile (m), botte (f)	[ba'rilɛ], ['bɔttɛ]
basin (for washing)	catino (m)	[ka'tinɔ]

tank (for liquid, gas)	**serbatoio** (m)	[sɛrba'tojo]
hip flask	**fiaschetta** (f)	[fias'ketta]
jerrycan	**tanica** (f)	['tanika]
cistern (tank)	**cisterna** (f)	[ʧis'tɛrna]

mug	**tazza** (f)	['tatʦa]
cup (of coffee, etc.)	**tazzina** (f)	[ta'ʦina]
saucer	**piattino** (m)	[pjat'tino]
glass (tumbler)	**bicchiere** (m)	[bik'kjerɛ]
glass (~ of vine)	**calice** (m)	['kaliʧe]
stew pot	**casseruola** (f)	[kassɛru'ɔʎa]

bottle (~ of wine)	**bottiglia** (f)	[bot'tiʎja]
neck (of the bottle)	**collo** (m)	['kɔllɔ]

carafe	**caraffa** (f)	[ka'raffa]
jug (earthenware)	**brocca** (f)	['brɔkka]
vessel (container)	**recipiente** (m)	[rɛʧipi'entɛ]
pot (crock)	**vaso** (m) **di coccio**	['vazɔ di 'kɔʧɔ]
vase	**vaso** (m)	['vazɔ]

bottle (~ of perfume)	**boccetta** (f)	[bo'ʧetta]
vial, small bottle	**fiala** (f)	[fi'aʎa]
tube (of toothpaste)	**tubetto** (m)	[tu'bɛttɔ]

sack (bag)	**sacco** (m)	['sakkɔ]
bag (paper ~, plastic ~)	**sacchetto** (m)	[sak'kɛttɔ]
packet (of cigarettes, etc.)	**pacchetto** (m)	[pak'kɛttɔ]

box (e.g. shoebox)	**scatola** (f)	['skatoʎa]
crate	**cassa** (f)	['kassa]
basket	**cesta** (f)	['ʧesta]

MAIN VERBS

13. The most important verbs. Part 1

to advise (vt)	consigliare (vt)	[kɔnsiˈʎjarɛ]
to agree (say yes)	essere d'accordo	[ˈɛssɛrɛ dakˈkɔrdɔ]
to answer (vi, vt)	rispondere (vi, vt)	[risˈpɔndɛrɛ]
to apologize (vi)	scusarsi (vr)	[skuˈzarsi]
to arrive (vi)	arrivare (vi)	[arriˈvarɛ]
to ask (~ oneself)	chiedere, domandare	[ˈkjedɛrɛ], [dɔmanˈdarɛ]
to ask (~ sb to do sth)	chiedere, domandare	[ˈkjedɛrɛ], [dɔmanˈdarɛ]
to be (vi)	essere (vi)	[ˈɛssɛrɛ]
to be afraid	avere paura	[aˈvɛrɛ paˈura]
to be hungry	avere fame	[aˈvɛrɛ ˈfamɛ]
to be interested in …	interessarsi di …	[intɛrɛsˈsarsi di]
to be needed	occorrere	[ɔkˈkɔrrɛrɛ]
to be surprised	stupirsi (vr)	[stuˈpirsi]
to be thirsty	avere sete	[aˈvɛrɛ ˈsɛtɛ]
to begin (vt)	cominciare (vt)	[kɔminˈʧarɛ]
to belong to …	appartenere (vi)	[appartɛˈnɛrɛ]
to boast (vi)	vantarsi (vr)	[vanˈtarsi]
to break (split into pieces)	rompere (vt)	[ˈrɔmpɛrɛ]
to call (for help)	chiamare (vt)	[kjaˈmarɛ]
can (v aux)	potere (v aux)	[pɔˈtɛrɛ]
to catch (vt)	afferrare (vt)	[afferˈrarɛ]
to change (vt)	cambiare (vt)	[kamˈbjarɛ]
to choose (select)	scegliere (vt)	[ˈʃeʎjerɛ]
to come down	scendere (vi)	[ˈʃendɛrɛ]
to come in (enter)	entrare (vi)	[ɛntˈrarɛ]
to compare (vt)	comparare (vt)	[kɔmpaˈrarɛ]
to complain (vi, vt)	lamentarsi (vr)	[ʎamɛnˈtarsi]
to confuse (mix up)	confondere (vt)	[kɔnˈfɔndɛrɛ]
to continue (vt)	continuare (vt)	[kɔntinuˈarɛ]
to control (vt)	controllare (vt)	[kɔntrɔˈʎarɛ]
to cook (dinner)	cucinare (vi)	[kuʧiˈnarɛ]
to cost (vt)	costare (vt)	[kɔsˈtarɛ]
to count (add up)	contare (vt)	[kɔnˈtarɛ]
to count on …	contare su …	[kɔnˈtarɛ su]
to create (vt)	creare (vt)	[krɛˈarɛ]
to cry (weep)	piangere (vi)	[ˈpjanʤɛrɛ]

14. The most important verbs. Part 2

to deceive (vi, vt)	ingannare (vt)	[iŋa'ŋarɛ]
to decorate (tree, street)	decorare (vt)	[dɛkɔ'rarɛ]
to defend (a country, etc.)	difendere (vt)	[di'fɛndɛrɛ]
to demand (request firmly)	esigere (vt)	[ɛ'zidʒɛrɛ]
to dig (vt)	scavare (vt)	[ska'varɛ]
to discuss (vt)	discutere (vt)	[dis'kutɛrɛ]
to do (vt)	fare (vt)	['farɛ]
to doubt (have doubts)	dubitare (vi)	[dubi'tarɛ]
to drop (let fall)	lasciar cadere	[ʎa'ʃar ka'dɛrɛ]
to excuse (forgive)	battaglia (f)	[bat'taʎja]
to exist (vi)	esistere (vi)	[ɛ'zistɛrɛ]
to expect (foresee)	prevedere (vt)	[prɛvɛ'dɛrɛ]
to explain (vt)	spiegare (vt)	[spjɛ'garɛ]
to fall (vi)	cadere (vi)	[ka'dɛrɛ]
to fancy (vt)	piacere (vi)	[pja'tʃɛrɛ]
to find (vt)	trovare (vt)	[trɔ'varɛ]
to finish (vt)	finire (vt)	[fi'nirɛ]
to fly (vi)	volare (vi)	[vɔ'ʎarɛ]
to follow … (come after)	seguire (vt)	[sɛgu'irɛ]
to forget (vi, vt)	dimenticare (vt)	[dimɛnti'karɛ]
to forgive (vt)	perdonare (vt)	[pɛrdɔ'narɛ]
to give (vt)	dare (vt)	['darɛ]
to give a hint	dare un suggerimento	[darɛ un sudʒeri'mɛntɔ]
to go (on foot)	andare (vi)	[an'darɛ]
to go for a swim	fare il bagno	['farɛ iʎ 'baɲɔ]
to go out (from …)	uscire (vi)	[u'ʃirɛ]
to guess right	indovinare (vt)	[indɔwi'narɛ]
to have (vt)	avere (vt)	[a'vɛrɛ]
to have breakfast	fare colazione	['farɛ kɔʎa'tsɔnɛ]
to have dinner	cenare (vi)	[tʃe'narɛ]
to have lunch	pranzare (vi)	[pran'tsarɛ]
to hear (vt)	sentire (vt)	[sɛn'tirɛ]
to help (vt)	aiutare (vt)	[aju'tarɛ]
to hide (vt)	nascondere (vt)	[nas'kondɛrɛ]
to hope (vi, vt)	sperare (vi, vt)	[spɛ'rarɛ]
to hunt (vi, vt)	cacciare (vt)	[ka'tʃarɛ]
to hurry (vi)	avere fretta	[a'vɛrɛ 'frɛtta]

15. The most important verbs. Part 3

to inform (vt)	informare (vt)	[infɔr'marɛ]
to insist (vi, vt)	insistere (vi)	[in'sistɛrɛ]
to insult (vt)	insultare (vt)	[insuʎ'tarɛ]
to invite (vt)	invitare (vt)	[inwi'tarɛ]

to joke (vi)	scherzare (vi)	[skɛr'tsarɛ]
to keep (vt)	conservare (vt)	[konsɛr'varɛ]
to keep silent	tacere (vi)	[ta'tʃerɛ]
to kill (vt)	uccidere (vt)	[u'tʃidɛrɛ]
to know (sb)	conoscere	[ko'noʃɛrɛ]
to know (sth)	sapere (vt)	[sa'pɛrɛ]

to laugh (vi)	ridere (vi)	['ridɛrɛ]
to liberate (city, etc.)	liberare (vt)	[libɛ'rarɛ]
to look for ... (search)	cercare (vt)	[tʃer'karɛ]
to love (sb)	amare qn	[a'marɛ]

to make a mistake	sbagliare (vi)	[zba'ʎjarɛ]
to manage, to run	dirigere (vt)	[di'ridʒerɛ]
to mean (signify)	significare (vt)	[siɲˈlifi'karɛ]
to mention (talk about)	menzionare (vt)	[mentsɨo'narɛ]
to miss (school, etc.)	mancare le lezioni	[ma'ŋkarɛ le le'tsɨoni]
to notice (see)	accorgersi (vr)	[ak'kordʒersi]

to object (vi, vt)	obiettare (vt)	[objet'tarɛ]
to observe (see)	osservare (vt)	[ɔssɛr'varɛ]
to open (vt)	aprire (vt)	[ap'rirɛ]
to order (meal, etc.)	ordinare (vt)	[ɔrdi'narɛ]
to order (mil.)	ordinare (vt)	[ɔrdi'narɛ]
to own (possess)	possedere (vt)	[pɔssɛ'dɛrɛ]

to participate (vi)	partecipare (vi)	[partɛtʃi'parɛ]
to pay (vi, vt)	pagare (vi, vt)	[pa'garɛ]
to permit (vt)	permettere (vt)	[pɛr'mɛttɛrɛ]
to plan (vt)	pianificare (vt)	[pjanifi'karɛ]
to play (children)	giocare (vi)	[dʒo'karɛ]
to pray (vi, vt)	pregare (vi, vt)	[prɛ'garɛ]
to prefer (vt)	preferire (vt)	[prɛfɛ'rirɛ]

to promise (vt)	promettere (vt)	[pro'mɛttɛrɛ]
to pronounce (vt)	pronunciare (vt)	[pronun'tʃarɛ]
to propose (vt)	proporre (vt)	[pro'pɔrrɛ]
to punish (vt)	punire (vt)	[pu'nirɛ]
to read (vi, vt)	leggere (vi, vt)	['ledʒerɛ]
to recommend (vt)	raccomandare (vt)	[rakkoman'darɛ]

to refuse (vi, vt)	rifiutarsi (vr)	[rifjy'tarsi]
to regret (be sorry)	rincrescere (vi)	[riŋk'rɛʃɛrɛ]
to rent (sth from sb)	affittare (vt)	[affit'tarɛ]
to repeat (say again)	ripetere (vt)	[ri'pɛtɛrɛ]
to reserve, to book	riservare (vt)	[risɛr'varɛ]
to run (vi)	correre (vi)	['kɔrrɛrɛ]

16. The most important verbs. Part 4

to save (rescue)	salvare (vt)	[saʎ'varɛ]
to say (~ thank you)	dire (vt)	['dirɛ]
to scold (vt)	sgridare (vt)	[zgri'darɛ]
to see (vt)	vedere (vt)	[vɛ'dɛrɛ]

to sell (vt)	**vendere** (vt)	['vɛndɛrɛ]
to send (vt)	**mandare** (vt)	[man'darɛ]
to shoot (vi)	**sparare** (vi)	[spa'rarɛ]
to shout (vi)	**gridare** (vi)	[gri'darɛ]
to show (vt)	**mostrare** (vt)	[mɔst'rarɛ]

to sign (document)	**firmare** (vt)	[fir'marɛ]
to sit down (vi)	**sedersi** (vr)	[sɛ'dɛrsi]
to smile (vi)	**sorridere** (vi)	[sɔr'ridɛrɛ]
to speak (vi, vt)	**parlare** (vi, vt)	[par'ʎarɛ]

to steal (money, etc.)	**rubare** (vt)	[ru'barɛ]
to stop (cease)	**cessare** (vt)	[ʧes'sarɛ]
to stop (for pause, etc.)	**fermarsi** (vr)	[fɛr'marsi]
to study (vt)	**studiare** (vt)	[studi'arɛ]
to swim (vi)	**nuotare** (vi)	[nuɔ'tarɛ]

to take (vt)	**prendere** (vt)	['prɛndɛrɛ]
to think (vi, vt)	**pensare** (vi, vt)	[pɛn'sarɛ]
to threaten (vt)	**minacciare** (vt)	[mina'ʧarɛ]
to touch (by hands)	**toccare** (vt)	[tɔk'karɛ]
to translate (vt)	**tradurre** (vt)	[tra'durrɛ]
to trust (vt)	**fidarsi** (vr)	[fi'darsi]
to try (attempt)	**tentare** (vt)	[tɛn'tarɛ]
to turn (~ to the left)	**girare** (vi)	[ʤi'rarɛ]

to underestimate (vt)	**sottovalutare** (vt)	[sɔttɔvaly'tarɛ]
to understand (vt)	**capire** (vt)	[ka'pirɛ]
to unite (vt)	**unire** (vt)	[u'nirɛ]
to wait (vt)	**aspettare** (vt)	[aspɛt'tarɛ]
to want (wish, desire)	**volere** (vt)	[vɔ'lerɛ]
to warn (vt)	**avvertire** (vt)	[avwer'tirɛ]
to work (vi)	**lavorare** (vi)	[ʎavɔ'rarɛ]
to write (vt)	**scrivere** (vt)	['skrivɛrɛ]
to write down	**annotare** (vt)	[aŋɔ'tarɛ]

TIME. CALENDAR

17. Weekdays

Monday	**lunedì** (m)	[lyne'di]
Tuesday	**martedì** (m)	[martɛ'di]
Wednesday	**mercoledì** (m)	[mɛrkole'di]
Thursday	**giovedì** (m)	[dʒɔve'di]
Friday	**venerdì** (m)	[vɛnɛr'di]
Saturday	**sabato** (m)	['sabatɔ]
Sunday	**domenica** (f)	[dɔ'mɛnika]
today (adv)	**oggi**	['ɔdʒi]
tomorrow (adv)	**domani**	[dɔ'mani]
the day after tomorrow	**dopo domani**	['dɔpɔ dɔ'mani]
yesterday (adv)	**ieri**	['jeri]
the day before yesterday	**l'altro ieri**	['ʎaʎtrɔ 'jeri]
day	**giorno** (m)	['dʒɔrnɔ]
working day	**giorno** (m) **lavorativo**	['dʒɔrnɔ ʎavɔra'tivɔ]
public holiday	**giorno** (m) **festivo**	['dʒɔrnɔ fɛs'tivɔ]
day off	**giorno** (m) **di riposo**	['dʒɔrnɔ di ri'pɔzɔ]
weekend	**fine** (m) **settimana**	['finɛ sɛtti'mana]
all day long	**tutto il giorno**	['tuttɔ iʎ 'dʒɔrnɔ]
next day (adv)	**l'indomani**	[lindɔ'mani]
two days ago	**due giorni fa**	['duɛ 'dʒɔrni fa]
the day before	**il giorno prima**	[iʎ 'dʒɔrnɔ 'prima]
daily (adj)	**quotidiano**	[kuɔtidi'anɔ]
every day (adv)	**ogni giorno**	['ɔɲi 'dʒɔrnɔ]
week	**settimana** (f)	[sɛtti'mana]
last week (adv)	**la settimana scorsa**	[ʎa sɛtti'mana 'skɔrsa]
next week (adv)	**la settimana prossima**	[ʎa sɛtti'mana 'prɔssima]
weekly (adj)	**settimanale**	[sɛttima'nale]
every week (adv)	**ogni settimana**	[ɔɲi sɛtti'mana]
twice a week	**due volte alla settimana**	['duɛ 'vɔʎtɛ 'aʎa sɛtti'mana]
every Tuesday	**ogni martedì**	['ɔɲi marte'di]

18. Hours. Day and night

morning	**mattina** (f)	[mat'tina]
in the morning	**di mattina**	[di mat'tina]
noon, midday	**mezzogiorno** (m)	[mɛdzo'dʒɔrnɔ]
in the afternoon	**nel pomeriggio**	[neʎ pɔmɛ'ridʒɔ]
evening	**sera** (f)	['sɛra]
in the evening	**di sera**	[di 'sɛra]

night	notte (f)	['nɔttɛ]
at night	di notte	[di 'nɔttɛ]
midnight	mezzanotte (f)	[mɛʤa'nɔttɛ]

second	secondo (m)	[sɛ'kɔndɔ]
minute	minuto (m)	[mi'nutɔ]
hour	ora (f)	['ɔra]
half an hour	mezzora (f)	[mɛ'ʣora]
quarter of an hour	un quarto d'ora	[un ku'artɔ 'dɔra]
fifteen minutes	quindici minuti	[ku'indiʧi mi'nuti]
24 hours	ventiquattro ore	[vɛntiku'attrɔ 'ɔrɛ]

sunrise	levata (f) del sole	[le'vata dɛʎ 'sɔle]
dawn	alba (f)	['aʎba]
early morning	mattutino (m)	[mattu'tinɔ]
sunset	tramonto (m)	[tra'mɔntɔ]

early in the morning	di buon mattino	[di bu'ɔn mat'tinɔ]
this morning	stamattina	[stamat'tina]
tomorrow morning	domattina	[dɔmat'tina]

this afternoon	oggi pomeriggio	['ɔʤi pɔmɛ'riʤɔ]
in the afternoon	nel pomeriggio	[nɛʎ pɔmɛ'riʤɔ]
tomorrow afternoon	domani pomeriggio	[dɔ'mani pɔmɛ'riʤɔ]

| tonight (this evening) | stasera | [sta'sɛra] |
| tomorrow night | domani sera | [dɔ'mani 'sɛra] |

at 3 o'clock sharp	alle tre precise	['alle trɛ prɛ'ʧizɛ]
about 4 o'clock	verso le quattro	['vɛrsɔ le ku'attrɔ]
by 12 o'clock	per le dodici	[pɛr le 'dɔdiʧi]

in 20 minutes	fra venti minuti	[fra 'vɛnti mi'nuti]
in an hour	fra un'ora	[fra un 'ɔra]
on time (adv)	puntualmente	[puntuaʎ'mentɛ]

a quarter to ...	un quarto di ...	[un ku'artɔ di]
within an hour	entro un'ora	['ɛntrɔ un 'ɔra]
every 15 minutes	ogni quindici minuti	['ɔɲi ku'indiʧi mi'nuti]
round the clock	giorno e notte	['ʤɔrnɔ ɛ 'nɔttɛ]

19. Months. Seasons

January	gennaio (m)	[ʤe'ŋajo]
February	febbraio (m)	[fɛbb'rajo]
March	marzo (m)	['marʦɔ]
April	aprile (m)	[ap'rile]
May	maggio (m)	['maʤɔ]
June	giugno (m)	['ʤuɲɔ]

July	luglio (m)	['lyʎɔ]
August	agosto (m)	[a'gostɔ]
September	settembre (m)	[sɛt'tɛmbrɛ]
October	ottobre (m)	[ɔt'tɔbrɛ]

| November | novembre (m) | [nɔ'vɛmbrɛ] |
| December | dicembre (m) | [di'tʃembrɛ] |

spring	primavera (f)	[prima'vɛra]
in spring	in primavera	[in prima'vɛra]
spring (as adj)	primaverile	[primavɛ'rile]

summer	estate (f)	[ɛs'tatɛ]
in summer	in estate	[in ɛs'tatɛ]
summer (as adj)	estivo	[ɛs'tivɔ]

autumn	autunno (m)	[au'tuŋɔ]
in autumn	in autunno	[in au'tuŋɔ]
autumn (as adj)	autunnale	[autu'ŋale]

winter	inverno (m)	[in'vɛrnɔ]
in winter	in inverno	[in in'vɛrnɔ]
winter (as adj)	invernale	[invɛr'nale]

month	mese (m)	['mezɛ]
this month	questo mese	[ku'ɛstɔ 'mɛzɛ]
next month	il mese prossimo	[iʎ 'mɛzɛ 'prɔssimɔ]
last month	il mese scorso	[iʎ 'mɛzɛ 'skɔrsɔ]

a month ago	un mese fa	[un 'mɛzɛ fa]
in a month	fra un mese	[fra un 'mɛzɛ]
in two months	fra due mesi	[fra 'duɛ 'mɛzi]
a whole month	un mese intero	[un 'mɛzɛ in'tɛrɔ]
all month long	per tutto il mese	[per 'tuttɔ iʎ 'mɛzɛ]

monthly (~ magazine)	mensile	[men'sile]
monthly (adv)	mensilmente	[mensiʎ'mɛntɛ]
every month	ogni mese	['ɔɲi 'mɛzɛ]
twice a month	due volte al mese	['duɛ 'vɔʎtɛ aʎ 'mɛzɛ]

year	anno (m)	['aŋɔ]
this year	quest'anno	[kuɛs'taŋɔ]
next year	l'anno prossimo	['ʎaŋɔ 'prɔssimɔ]
last year	l'anno scorso	['ʎaŋɔ 'skɔrsɔ]

a year ago	un anno fa	[un 'aŋɔ fa]
in a year	fra un anno	[fra un 'aŋɔ]
in two years	fra due anni	[fra 'duɛ 'aɲi]
a whole year	un anno intero	[un 'aŋɔ in'tɛrɔ]
all year long	per tutto l'anno	[per 'tuttɔ 'ʎaŋɔ]

every year	ogni anno	['ɔɲi 'aŋɔ]
annual (adj)	annuale	[aŋu'ale]
annually (adv)	annualmente	[aŋuaʎ'mɛntɛ]
4 times a year	quattro volte all'anno	[ku'attrɔ 'vɔʎtɛ a'ʎaŋɔ]

date (e.g. today's ~)	data (f)	['data]
date (e.g. ~ of birth)	data (f)	['data]
calendar	calendario (m)	[kalen'dariɔ]
half a year	mezz'anno (m)	[mɛ'dzaŋɔ]
six months	semestre (m)	[sɛ'mɛstrɛ]

| season (summer, etc.) | **stagione** (f) | [sta'dʒɔnɛ] |
| century | **secolo** (m) | ['sɛkɔlɔ] |

TRAVEL. HOTEL

20. Trip. Travel

tourism	turismo (m)	[tu'rizmɔ]
tourist	turista (m)	[tu'rista]
trip, voyage	viaggio (m)	['vjadʒɔ]
adventure	avventura (f)	[avvɛn'tura]
trip, journey	viaggio (m)	['vjadʒɔ]
holiday	vacanza (f)	[va'kantsa]
to be on holiday	essere in vacanza	['ɛssɛrɛ in va'kantsa]
rest	riposo (m)	[ri'pozɔ]
train	treno (m)	['trɛnɔ]
by train	in treno	[in 'trɛnɔ]
aeroplane	aereo (m)	[a'ɛrɛɔ]
by aeroplane	in aereo	[in a'ɛrɛɔ]
by car	in macchina	[in 'makkina]
by ship	in nave	[in 'navɛ]
luggage	bagaglio (m)	[ba'gaʎɔ]
suitcase, luggage	valigia (f)	[va'lidʒa]
luggage trolley	carrello (m)	[kar'rɛllɔ]
passport	passaporto (m)	[passa'portɔ]
visa	visto (m)	['wistɔ]
ticket	biglietto (m)	[bi'ʎjettɔ]
air ticket	biglietto (m) aereo	[bi'ʎjettɔ a'ɛrɛɔ]
guidebook	guida (f)	[gu'ida]
map	carta (f) geografica	['karta dʒeɔg'rafika]
area (rural ~)	località (f)	[lɔkali'ta]
place, site	luogo (m)	[ly'ɔgɔ]
exotica	ogetti (m pl) esotici	[ɔ'dʒetti ɛ'zɔtitʃi]
exotic (adj)	esotico	[ɛ'zɔtikɔ]
amazing (adj)	sorprendente	[sɔrprɛn'dɛntɛ]
group	gruppo (m)	['gruppɔ]
excursion	escursione (f)	[ɛskursi'ɔnɛ]
guide (person)	guida (f)	[gu'ida]

21. Hotel

hotel, inn	battaglia (f)	[bat'taʎja]
hotel	albergo, hotel (m)	[aʎ'bɛrgɔ], [ɔ'tɛʎ]
motel	motel (m)	[mɔ'tɛʎ]

three-star (adj)	tre stelle	['trɛ 'stɛlle]
five-star	cinque stelle	['tʃiŋkuɛ 'stɛlle]
to stay (in hotel, etc.)	alloggiare (vi)	[allɔ'dʒarɛ]

room	camera (f)	['kamɛra]
single room	camera (f) singola	['kamɛra 'siŋɔʎa]
double room	camera (f) doppia	['kamɛra 'dɔppia]
to book a room	prenotare una camera	[prɛnɔ'tarɛ una 'kamɛra]

| half board | mezza pensione (f) | ['mɛdza pɛnsi'ɔnɛ] |
| full board | pensione (f) completa | [pɛnsi'ɔnɛ kɔmp'leta] |

with bath	con bagno	[kɔn 'baɲɔ]
with shower	con doccia	[kɔn 'dɔtʃa]
satellite television	televisione (f) satellitare	[tɛlewizi'ɔnɛ satɛlli'tarɛ]
air-conditioner	condizionatore (m)	[kɔnditsiona'torɛ]
towel	asciugamano (m)	[aʃuga'manɔ]
key	chiave (f)	['kjavɛ]

administrator	amministratore (m)	[amministra'torɛ]
chambermaid	cameriera (f)	[kamɛ'rjera]
porter, bellboy	portabagagli (m)	[portaba'gaʎi]
doorman	portiere (m)	[por'tʲerɛ]

restaurant	ristorante (m)	[risto'rantɛ]
pub, bar	bar (m)	[bar]
breakfast	colazione (f)	[koʎa'tsʲonɛ]
dinner	cena (f)	['tʃena]
buffet	buffet (m)	[buf'fɛ]

| lobby | hall (f) | [ɔʎ] |
| lift | ascensore (m) | [aʃɛn'sorɛ] |

| DO NOT DISTURB | NON DISTURBARE | [nɔn distur'barɛ] |
| NO SMOKING | VIETATO FUMARE! | [vje'tato fu'marɛ] |

22. Sightseeing

monument	monumento (m)	[mɔnu'mɛntɔ]
fortress	fortezza (f)	[for'tɛtsa]
palace	palazzo (m)	[pa'ʎatsɔ]
castle	castello (m)	[kas'tɛllɔ]
tower	torre (f)	['torrɛ]
mausoleum	mausoleo (m)	[mauzo'leo]

architecture	architettura (f)	[arkitɛt'tura]
medieval (adj)	medievale	[mɛdiɛ'vale]
ancient (adj)	antico	[an'tiko]
national (adj)	nazionale	[natsio'nale]
well-known (adj)	famoso	[fa'mɔzo]

tourist	turista (m)	[tu'rista]
guide (person)	guida (f)	[gu'ida]
excursion	escursione (f)	[ɛskursi'ɔnɛ]

to show (vt)	**fare vedere**	['farɛ vɛ'dɛrɛ]
to tell (vt)	**raccontare** (vt)	[rakkɔn'tarɛ]
to find (vt)	**trovare** (vt)	[trɔ'varɛ]
to get lost	**perdersi** (vr)	['pɛrdɛrsi]
map (e.g. underground ~)	**mappa** (f)	['mappa]
map (e.g. city ~)	**piantina** (f)	[pjan'tina]
souvenir, gift	**souvenir** (m)	[suvɛ'nir]
gift shop	**negozio** (m) **di articoli da regalo**	[nɛ'gɔtsiɔ di ar'tikɔli da rɛ'galɔ]
to take pictures	**fare foto**	['farɛ 'fɔtɔ]
to be photographed	**farsi fotografare**	['farsi fɔtɔgra'farɛ]

TRANSPORT

23. Airport

airport	**aeroporto** (m)	[aɛrɔ'pɔrtɔ]
aeroplane	**aereo** (m)	[a'ɛrɛɔ]
airline	**compagnia** (f) **aerea**	[kɔmpa'nia a'ɛrɛa]
air-traffic controller	**controllore** (m) **di volo**	[kɔntrɔl'lɔrɛ di 'vɔlɔ]
departure	**partenza** (f)	[par'tɛntsa]
arrival	**arrivo** (m)	[ar'rivɔ]
to arrive (by plane)	**arrivare** (vi)	[arri'varɛ]
departure time	**ora** (f) **di partenza**	['ɔra di par'tɛntsa]
arrival time	**ora** (f) **di arrivo**	['ɔra di ar'rivɔ]
to be delayed	**essere ritardato**	['ɛssɛrɛ ritar'datɔ]
flight delay	**volo** (m) **ritardato**	['vɔlɔ ritar'datɔ]
information board	**tabellone** (m) **orari**	[tabɛl'lɔnɛ ɔ'rari]
information	**informazione** (f)	[infɔrma'tsjɔnɛ]
to announce (vt)	**annunciare** (vt)	[anun'tʃarɛ]
flight (e.g. next ~)	**volo** (m)	['vɔlɔ]
customs	**dogana** (f)	[dɔ'gana]
customs officer	**doganiere** (m)	[dɔga'njerɛ]
customs declaration	**dichiarazione** (f)	[dikjara'tsjɔnɛ]
to fill in the declaration	**riempire una dichiarazione**	[riɛm'pirɛ una dikjara'tsjɔnɛ]
passport control	**controllo** (m) **passaporti**	[kɔnt'rɔllɔ passa'pɔrti]
luggage	**bagaglio** (m)	[ba'gaʎɔ]
hand luggage	**bagaglio** (m) **a mano**	[ba'gaʎɔ a 'manɔ]
Lost Luggage Desk	**Assistenza bagagli**	[asis'tɛntsa ba'gaʎi]
luggage trolley	**carrello** (m)	[kar'rɛllɔ]
landing	**atterraggio** (m)	[attɛr'radʒɔ]
landing strip	**pista** (f) **di atterraggio**	['pista di attɛr'radʒɔ]
to land (vi)	**atterrare** (vi)	[attɛr'rarɛ]
airstairs	**scaletta** (f) **dell'aereo**	[ska'letta dɛʎ a'ɛrɛɔ]
check-in	**check-in** (m)	[tʃɛ'kin]
check-in desk	**banco** (m) **del check-in**	['baŋkɔ dɛʎ tʃɛ'kin]
to check-in (vi)	**fare il check-in**	['farɛ iʎ tʃɛ'kin]
boarding pass	**carta** (f) **d'imbarco**	['karta dim'barkɔ]
departure gate	**porta** (f) **d'imbarco**	['pɔrta dim'barkɔ]
transit	**transito** (m)	['tranzitɔ]
to wait (vt)	**aspettare** (vt)	[aspɛt'tarɛ]
departure lounge	**sala** (f) **d'attesa**	['saʎa dat'tɛza]

| to see off | accompagnare (vt) | [akkɔmpa'ɲjarɛ] |
| to say goodbye | congedarsi (vr) | [kɔndʒe'darsi] |

24. Aeroplane

aeroplane	aereo (m)	[a'ɛrɛɔ]
air ticket	biglietto (m) aereo	[bi'ʎjettɔ a'ɛrɛɔ]
airline	compagnia (f) aerea	[kɔmpa'nia a'ɛrɛa]
airport	aeroporto (m)	[aɛrɔ'pɔrtɔ]
supersonic (adj)	supersonico	[supɛr'sɔnikɔ]

captain	comandante (m)	[kɔman'dantɛ]
crew	equipaggio (m)	[ɛkui'padʒɔ]
pilot	pilota (m)	[pi'lɔta]
stewardess	hostess (f)	['ɔstɛss]
navigator	navigatore (m)	[nawiga'tɔrɛ]

wings	ali (f pl)	['ali]
tail	coda (f)	['kɔda]
cockpit	cabina (f)	[ka'bina]
engine	motore (m)	[mɔ'tɔrɛ]
undercarriage	carrello (m) d'atterraggio	[kar'rɛllɔ dattɛr'radʒɔ]
turbine	turbina (f)	[tur'bina]
propeller	elica (f)	['ɛlika]
black box	scatola (f) nera	['skatɔʎa 'nɛra]
control column	barra (f) di comando	['barra di kɔ'mandɔ]
fuel	combustibile (m)	[kɔmbus'tibile]

safety card	safety card (f)	['sɛjfti kard]
oxygen mask	maschera (f) ad ossigeno	['maskɛra ad ɔs'sidʒenɔ]
uniform	uniforme (f)	[uni'fɔrmɛ]
lifejacket	giubbotto (m) di salvataggio	[dʒub'bɔttɔ di saʎva'tadʒɔ]
parachute	paracadute (m)	[paraka'dutɛ]
takeoff	decollo (m)	[dɛ'kɔllɔ]
to take off (vi)	decollare (vi)	[dɛkɔ'ʎarɛ]
runway	pista (f) di decollo	['pista di dɛ'kɔllɔ]

visibility	visibilità (f)	[wizibili'ta]
flight (act of flying)	volo (m)	['vɔlɔ]
altitude	altitudine (f)	[aʎti'tudinɛ]
air pocket	vuoto (m) d'aria	[vu'ɔtɔ 'daria]

seat	posto (m)	['pɔstɔ]
headphones	cuffia (f)	['kuffʲa]
folding tray	tavolinetto (m) pieghevole	[tavoli'nɛttɔ pje'gɛvole]
airplane window	oblò (m), finestrino (m)	[ɔb'lɔ], [finest'rinɔ]
aisle	corridoio (m)	[kɔrri'dɔjo]

25. Train

| train | treno (m) | ['trɛnɔ] |
| suburban train | elettrotreno (m) | [ɛlettrɔt'rɛnɔ] |

fast train	treno (m) rapido	['trɛno 'rapido]
diesel locomotive	locomotiva (f) diesel	[lɔkɔmo'tiva 'dizɛʎ]
steam engine	locomotiva (f) a vapore	[lɔkɔmo'tiva a va'pɔrɛ]

| coach, carriage | carrozza (f) | [kar'rɔtsa] |
| restaurant car | vagone (m) ristorante | [va'gɔnɛ risto'rantɛ] |

rails	rotaie (f pl)	[rɔ'taje]
railway	ferrovia (f)	[fɛrro'wia]
sleeper (track support)	traversa (f)	[tra'vɛrsa]

platform (railway ~)	banchina (f)	[ba'ŋkina]
platform (~ 1, 2, etc.)	binario (m)	[bi'nario]
semaphore	semaforo (m)	[sɛ'mafɔrɔ]
station	stazione (f)	[sta'tsⁱɔnɛ]
train driver	macchinista (m)	[makki'nista]
porter (of luggage)	portabagagli (m)	[portaba'gaʎi]
train steward	cuccettista (m, f)	[kutʃet'tista]
passenger	passeggero (m)	[passɛ'dʒero]
ticket inspector	controllore (m)	[kontrol'lɔrɛ]

| corridor (in train) | corridoio (m) | [korri'dojo] |
| emergency break | freno (m) di emergenza | ['frɛno di ɛmɛr'dʒentsa] |

compartment	scompartimento (m)	[skomparti'mɛnto]
berth	cuccetta (f)	[ku'tʃetta]
upper berth	cuccetta (f) superiore	[ku'tʃetta supɛri'ɔrɛ]
lower berth	cuccetta (f) inferiore	[ku'tʃetta infɛri'ɔrɛ]
linen	biancheria (f) da letto	[bⁱaŋke'ria da 'lɛtto]
ticket	biglietto (m)	[bi'ʎjetto]
timetable	orario (m)	[o'rario]
information display	tabellone (m) orari	[tabɛl'lɔnɛ o'rari]

to leave, to depart	partire (vi)	[par'tirɛ]
departure (of train)	partenza (f)	[par'tentsa]
to arrive (ab. train)	arrivare (vi)	[arri'varɛ]
arrival	arrivo (m)	[ar'rivo]

to arrive by train	arrivare con il treno	[arri'varɛ kon iʎ 'trɛno]
to get on the train	salire sul treno	[sa'lirɛ suʎ 'trɛno]
to get off the train	scendere dal treno	['ʃɛndɛrɛ daʎ 'trɛno]

| train crash | deragliamento (m) | [dɛraʎja'mɛnto] |
| to be derailed | deragliare (vi) | [dɛra'ʎjarɛ] |

steam engine	locomotiva (f) a vapore	[lɔkɔmo'tiva a va'pɔrɛ]
stoker, fireman	fuochista (m)	[fo'kista]
firebox	forno (m)	['forno]
coal	carbone (m)	[kar'bonɛ]

26. Ship

| ship | nave (f) | ['navɛ] |
| vessel | imbarcazione (f) | [imbarka'tsⁱɔnɛ] |

steamship	**piroscafo** (m)	[pi'rɔskafɔ]
riverboat	**barca** (f) **fluviale**	['barka fluwi'jale]
ocean liner	**transatlantico** (m)	[transat'lantikɔ]
cruiser	**incrociatore** (m)	[iŋkrɔtʃa'tɔrɛ]

yacht	**yacht** (m)	[jot]
tugboat	**rimorchiatore** (m)	[rimɔrkja'tɔrɛ]
barge	**chiatta** (f)	['kjatta]
ferry	**traghetto** (m)	[tra'gɛttɔ]

| sailing ship | **veliero** (m) | [vɛ'ʎjerɔ] |
| brigantine | **brigantino** (m) | [brigan'tinɔ] |

| ice breaker | **rompighiaccio** (m) | [rɔmpi'gjatʃɔ] |
| submarine | **sottomarino** (m) | [sɔttɔma'rinɔ] |

boat (flat-bottomed ~)	**barca** (f)	['barka]
dinghy	**scialuppa** (f)	[ʃa'luppa]
lifeboat	**scialuppa** (f) **di salvataggio**	[ʃa'lyppa di saʎva'tadʒɔ]
motorboat	**motoscafo** (m)	[mɔtɔs'kafɔ]

captain	**capitano** (m)	[kapi'tanɔ]
seaman	**marittimo** (m)	[ma'rittimɔ]
sailor	**marinaio** (m)	[mari'najo]
crew	**equipaggio** (m)	[ɛkui'padʒɔ]

boatswain	**nostromo** (m)	[nɔst'rɔmɔ]
ship's boy	**mozzo** (m) **di nave**	['mɔtsɔ di 'navɛ]
cook	**cuoco** (m)	[ku'ɔkɔ]
ship's doctor	**medico** (m) **di bordo**	['mɛdikɔ di 'bɔrdɔ]

deck	**ponte** (m)	['pɔntɛ]
mast	**albero** (m)	['aʎbɛrɔ]
sail	**vela** (f)	['vɛʎa]

hold	**stiva** (f)	['stiva]
bow (prow)	**prua** (f)	['prua]
stern	**poppa** (f)	['pɔppa]
oar	**remo** (m)	['rɛmɔ]
propeller	**elica** (f)	['ɛlika]

cabin	**cabina** (f)	[ka'bina]
wardroom	**quadrato** (m) **degli ufficiali**	[kuad'ratɔ dɛlli uffi'tʃali]
engine room	**sala** (f) **macchine**	['saʎa 'makkinɛ]
the bridge	**ponte** (m) **di comando**	['pɔntɛ di kɔ'mandɔ]
radio room	**cabina** (f) **radiotelegrafica**	[ka'bina radiɔtɛleg'rafika]
wave (radio)	**onda** (f)	['ɔnda]
logbook	**giornale** (m) **di bordo**	[dʒɔr'nale di 'bɔrdɔ]

spyglass	**cannocchiale** (m)	[kaŋɔk'kjale]
bell	**campana** (f)	[kam'pana]
flag	**bandiera** (f)	[ban'djera]

rope (mooring ~)	**cavo** (m) **d'ormeggio**	['kavɔ dɔr'medʒɔ]
knot (bowline, etc.)	**nodo** (m)	['nɔdɔ]
handrail	**ringhiera** (f)	[riŋʰ'era]

gangway	**passerella** (f)	[passɛ'rɛʎa]
anchor	**ancora** (f)	['aŋkɔra]
to weigh anchor	**levare l'ancora**	[le'varɛ 'ʎaŋkɔra]
to drop anchor	**gettare l'ancora**	[dʒet'tarɛ 'ʎaŋkɔra]
anchor chain	**catena** (f) **dell'ancora**	[ka'tɛna dɛʎ 'aŋkɔra]
port (harbour)	**porto** (m)	['pɔrtɔ]
wharf, quay	**banchina** (f)	[ba'ŋkina]
to berth (moor)	**ormeggiarsi** (vr)	[ɔrmɛ'dʒarsi]
to cast off	**salpare** (vi)	[saʎ'parɛ]
trip, voyage	**viaggio** (m)	['vjadʒɔ]
cruise (sea trip)	**crociera** (f)	[krɔ'tʃera]
course (route)	**rotta** (f)	['rɔtta]
route (itinerary)	**itinerario** (m)	[itinɛ'rariɔ]
fairway	**tratto** (m) **navigabile**	['trattɔ nawi'gabile]
shallows (shoal)	**secca** (f)	['sɛkka]
to run aground	**arenarsi** (vr)	[arɛ'narsi]
storm	**tempesta** (f)	[tɛm'pɛsta]
signal	**segnale** (m)	[sɛ'ɲjale]
to sink (vi)	**affondare** (vi)	[affɔn'darɛ]
Man overboard!	**Uomo in mare!**	[u'omɔ in 'marɛ]
SOS	**SOS**	['ɛssɛ ɔ 'ɛssɛ]
ring buoy	**salvagente** (m) **anulare**	[saʎva'dʒɛntɛ anu'larɛ]

CITY

27. Urban transport

bus, coach	autobus (m)	['autɔbus]
tram	tram (m)	[tram]
trolleybus	filobus (m)	['filɜbus]
route (of bus)	itinerario (m)	[itinɛ'rariɔ]
number (e.g. bus ~)	numero (m)	['numɛrɔ]
to go by ...	andare in ...	[an'darɛ in]
to get on (~ the bus)	salire su ...	[sa'lirɛ su]
to get off ...	scendere da ...	['ʃɛndɛrɛ da]
stop (e.g. bus ~)	fermata (f)	[fɛr'mata]
next stop	prossima fermata (f)	['prɔssima fɛr'mata]
terminus	capolinea (m)	[kapɔ'linɛa]
timetable	orario (m)	[ɔ'rariɔ]
to wait (vt)	aspettare (vt)	[aspɛt'tarɛ]
ticket	biglietto (m)	[bi'ʎjettɔ]
fare	prezzo (m) del biglietto	['prɛtsɔ dɛʎ bi'ʎjettɔ]
cashier	cassiere (m)	[kas'sjerɛ]
ticket inspection	controllo (m) dei biglietti	[kɔnt'rɔllɔ dei bi'ʎjeti]
inspector	bigliettaio (m)	[biʎjet'tajo]
to be late (for ...)	essere in ritardo	['ɛssɛrɛ in ri'tardɔ]
to miss (~ the train, etc.)	perdere (vt)	['pɛrdɛrɛ]
to be in a hurry	avere fretta	[a'vɛrɛ 'frɛtta]
taxi, cab	taxi (m)	['taksi]
taxi driver	taxista (m)	[tak'sista]
by taxi	in taxi	[in 'taksi]
taxi rank	parcheggio (m) di taxi	[par'kɛdʒɔ di 'taksi]
to call a taxi	chiamare un taxi	[kja'marɛ un 'taksi]
to take a taxi	prendere un taxi	['prɛndɛrɛ un 'taksi]
traffic	traffico (m)	['traffikɔ]
traffic jam	ingorgo (m)	[i'ŋɔrgɔ]
rush hour	ore (f pl) di punta	['ɔrɛ di 'punta]
to park (vi)	parcheggiarsi (vr)	[parkɛ'dʒarsi]
to park (vt)	parcheggiare (vt)	[parkɛ'dʒarɛ]
car park	parcheggio (m)	[par'kɛdʒɔ]
underground, tube	metropolitana (f)	[metrɔpɔli'tana]
station	stazione (f)	[sta'tsʲɔnɛ]
to take the tube	prendere la metropolitana	['prɛndɛrɛ ʎa metrɔpɔli'tana]
train	treno (m)	['trɛnɔ]
train station	stazione (f) ferroviaria	[sta'tsʲɔnɛ fɛrrɔ'vʲaria]

28. City. Life in the city

city, town	città (f)	[tʃit'ta]
capital	capitale (f)	[kapi'tale]
village	villaggio (m)	[wi'ʎadʒɔ]

city map	mappa (f) della città	['mappa 'dɛʎa tʃit'ta]
city centre	centro (m) della città	['tʃentrɔ 'dɛʎa tʃit'ta]
suburb	sobborgo (m)	[sɔb'bɔrgɔ]
suburban (adj)	suburbano	[subur'banɔ]

outskirts	periferia (f)	[pɛrife'ria]
environs (suburbs)	dintorni (m pl)	[din'tɔrni]
quarter	isolato (m)	[izɔ'ʎatɔ]
residential quarter	quartiere (m) residenziale	[kuar'tʲerɛ rɛzidɛntsi'ale]

traffic	traffico (m)	['traffikɔ]
traffic lights	semaforo (m)	[sɛ'mafɔrɔ]
public transport	trasporti (m pl) urbani	[tras'pɔrti ur'bani]
crossroads	incrocio (m)	[iŋk'rɔtʃɔ]

zebra crossing	passaggio (m) pedonale	[pas'sadʒɔ pɛdɔ'nale]
pedestrian subway	sottopassaggio (m)	[sɔttɔpas'sadʒɔ]
to cross (vt)	attraversare (vt)	[attravɛr'sarɛ]
pedestrian	pedone (m)	[pɛ'dɔnɛ]
pavement	marciapiede (m)	[martʃa'pjedɛ]

| bridge | ponte (m) | ['pɔntɛ] |
| embankment | banchina (f) | [ba'ŋkina] |

allée	vialetto (m)	[wia'lettɔ]
park	parco (m)	['parkɔ]
boulevard	boulevard (m)	[buʎ'var]
square	piazza (f)	['pjatsa]
avenue (wide street)	viale (m), corso (m)	[wi'alɛ], ['kɔrsɔ]
street	via (f), strada (f)	['wia], ['strada]
lane	vicolo (m)	['wikɔlɔ]
dead end	vicolo (m) cieco	['wikɔlɔ 'tʃjekɔ]

house	casa (f)	['kaza]
building	edificio (m)	[ɛdi'fitʃɔ]
skyscraper	grattacielo (m)	[gratta'tʃelɔ]

facade	facciata (f)	[fa'tʃata]
roof	tetto (m)	['tɛttɔ]
window	finestra (f)	[fi'nɛstra]
arch	arco (m)	['arkɔ]
column	colonna (f)	[kɔ'lɔŋa]
corner	angolo (m)	['aŋɔlɔ]

shop window	vetrina (f)	[vɛt'rina]
shop sign	insegna (f)	[in'sɛɲja]
poster	cartellone (m)	[kartɛl'lɔnɛ]
advertising poster	cartellone (m) pubblicitario	[kartɛl'lɔnɛ pubblitʃi'tariɔ]
hoarding	tabellone (m) pubblicitario	[tabɛl'lɔnɛ pubblitʃi'tariɔ]

rubbish	pattume (m), spazzatura (f)	[pat'tumɛ], [spatsa'tura]
rubbish bin	pattumiera (f)	[pattu'mjera]
to litter (vi)	sporcare (vi)	[spor'karɛ]
rubbish dump	discarica (f) di rifiuti	[dis'karika di ri'fjyti]

telephone box	cabina (f) telefonica	[ka'bina tɛle'fonika]
street light	lampione (m)	[lam'pionɛ]
bench (park ~)	panchina (f)	[pa'ŋkina]

policeman	poliziotto (m)	[politsi'otto]
police	polizia (f)	[poli'tsia]
beggar	mendicante (m)	[mendi'kantɛ]
homeless	barbone (m)	[bar'bonɛ]

29. Urban institutions

shop	negozio (m)	[nɛ'gotsio]
chemist, pharmacy	farmacia (f)	[farma'tʃia]
optician	ottica (f)	['ottika]
shopping centre	centro (m) commerciale	['tʃentro kommɛr'tʃale]
supermarket	supermercato (m)	[supɛrmɛr'kato]

bakery	panetteria (f)	[panɛttɛ'ria]
baker	fornaio (m)	[for'najo]
cake shop	pasticceria (f)	[pastitʃe'ria]
grocery shop	drogheria (f)	[drogɛ'ria]
butcher shop	macelleria (f)	[matʃelle'ria]

greengrocer	fruttivendolo (m)	[frutti'vɛndolo]
market	mercato (m)	[mɛr'kato]

coffee bar	caffè (m)	[kaf'fɛ]
restaurant	ristorante (m)	[risto'rantɛ]
pub	birreria (f), pub (m)	[birrɛ'ria], [pab]
pizzeria	pizzeria (f)	[pitsɛ'ria]

hairdresser	salone (m) di parrucchiere	[sa'lonɛ di parruk'kjerɛ]
post office	ufficio (m) postale	[uf'fitʃo pos'tale]
dry cleaners	lavanderia (f) a secco	[ʎavandɛ'ria a 'sɛkko]
photo studio	studio (m) fotografico	['studio fotog'rafiko]

shoe shop	negozio (m) di scarpe	[nɛ'gotsio di 'skarpɛ]
bookshop	libreria (f)	[librɛ'ria]
sports shop	negozio (m) sportivo	[nɛ'gotsio spor'tivo]

clothing repair	riparazione (f) di abiti	[ripara'tsionɛ di 'abiti]
formal wear hire	noleggio (m) di abiti	[no'ledʒo di 'abiti]
DVD rental shop	noleggio DVD (m)	[no'ledʒo divu'di]

circus	circo (m)	['tʃirko]
zoo	zoo (m)	['dzo:]
cinema	cinema (m)	['tʃinɛma]
museum	museo (m)	[mu'zɛo]
library	biblioteca (f)	[biblio'tɛka]

theatre	teatro (m)	[tɛ'atrɔ]
opera	teatro (m) dell'opera	[tɛ'atrɔ dɛʎ 'ɔpera]
nightclub	nightclub (m)	['najtklɛb]
casino	casinò (m)	[kazi'nɔ]

mosque	moschea (f)	[mɔs'kɛa]
synagogue	sinagoga (f)	[sina'gɔga]
cathedral	cattedrale (f)	[kattɛd'rale]
temple	tempio (m)	['tɛmpʲɔ]
church	chiesa (f)	['kjeza]

institute	istituto (m)	[isti'tutɔ]
university	università (f)	[univɛrsi'ta]
school	scuola (f)	[sku'ɔʎa]

prefecture	prefettura (f)	[prɛfɛt'tura]
town hall	municipio (m)	[muni'ʧipiɔ]
hotel	albergo (m)	[aʎ'bɛrgɔ]
bank	banca (f)	['baŋka]

embassy	ambasciata (f)	[amba'ʃata]
travel agency	agenzia (f) di viaggi	[adʒen'tsia di wi'jadʒi]
information office	ufficio (m) informazioni	[uf'fiʧɔ infɔrmatsi'ɔni]
money exchange	ufficio (m) dei cambi	[uf'fiʧɔ dɛi 'kambi]

underground, tube	metropolitana (f)	[metrɔpoli'tana]
hospital	ospedale (m)	[ɔspɛ'dale]

petrol station	distributore (m) di benzina	[distribu'tɔrɛ di ben'dzina]
car park	parcheggio (m)	[par'kɛdʒɔ]

30. Signs

shop sign	insegna (f)	[in'sɛɲja]
notice (written text)	iscrizione (f)	[iskri'tsʲɔnɛ]
poster	cartellone (m)	[kartɛl'lɔnɛ]
direction sign	segnale (m) di direzione	[se'ɲʲale di dirɛ'tsʲɔnɛ]
arrow (sign)	freccia (f)	['frɛʧa]

caution	avvertimento (m)	[avwerti'mɛntɔ]
warning sign	avvertimento (m)	[avwerti'mɛntɔ]
to warn (vt)	avvertire (vt)	[avwer'tirɛ]

closing day	giorno (m) di riposo	['dʒɔrnɔ di ri'pɔzɔ]
timetable (schedule)	orario (m)	[ɔ'rariɔ]
opening hours	orario (m) di apertura	[ɔ'rariɔ di apɛr'tura]

WELCOME!	BENVENUTI!	[bɛnvɛ'nuti]
ENTRANCE	ENTRATA	[ɛnt'rata]
WAY OUT	USCITA	[u'ʃita]

PUSH	SPINGERE	['spindʒerɛ]
PULL	TIRARE	[ti'rarɛ]
OPEN	APERTO	[a'pɛrtɔ]

CLOSED	CHIUSO	['kjyzɔ]
WOMEN	DONNE	['dɔŋɛ]
MEN	UOMINI	[u'omini]

DISCOUNTS	SCONTI	['skɔnti]
SALE	SALDI	['saʎdi]
NEW!	NOVITÀ!	[nɔwi'ta]
FREE	GRATIS	['gratis]

ATTENTION!	ATTENZIONE!	[attɛn'ʦʲɔnɛ]
NO VACANCIES	COMPLETO	[kɔmp'letɔ]
RESERVED	RISERVATO	[risɛr'vatɔ]

ADMINISTRATION	AMMINISTRAZIONE	[aministra'ʦʲɔnɛ]
STAFF ONLY	RISERVATO	[risɛr'vatɔ
	AL PERSONALE	aʎ pɛrsɔ'nale]

BEWARE OF THE DOG!	ATTENTI AL CANE	[at'tɛnti aʎ 'kanɛ]
NO SMOKING	VIETATO FUMARE!	[vje'tatɔ fu'marɛ]
DO NOT TOUCH!	NON TOCCARE!	[nɔn tɔk'karɛ]

DANGEROUS	PERICOLOSO	[pɛrikɔ'lɔzɔ]
DANGER	PERICOLO	[pɛ'rikɔlɔ]
HIGH TENSION	ALTA TENSIONE	['aʎta tɛnsi'ɔnɛ]
NO SWIMMING!	DIVIETO DI BALNEAZIONE	[di'vjetɔ di baʎnɛa'ʦʲɔnɛ]
OUT OF ORDER	GUASTO	[gu'astɔ]

FLAMMABLE	INFIAMMABILE	[infjam'mabile]
FORBIDDEN	VIETATO	[vje'tatɔ]
NO TRESPASSING!	VIETATO L'INGRESSO	[vje'tatɔ liŋ'rɛsɔ]
WET PAINT	VERNICE FRESCA	[vɛr'nitʃe 'frɛska]

31. Shopping

to buy (purchase)	comprare (vt)	[kɔmp'rarɛ]
purchase	acquisto (m)	[aku'istɔ]
to go shopping	fare acquisti	['farɛ aku'isti]
shopping	shopping (m)	['ʃɔppiŋ]

| to be open (ab. shop) | essere aperto | ['ɛssɛrɛ a'pɛrtɔ] |
| to be closed | essere chiuso | ['ɛssɛrɛ 'kjyzɔ] |

footwear	calzature (f pl)	[kaʎtsa'turɛ]
clothes, clothing	abbigliamento (m)	[abbiʎja'mɛntɔ]
cosmetics	cosmetica (f)	[kɔz'mɛtika]
food products	alimentari (m pl)	[alimɛn'tari]
gift, present	regalo (m)	[rɛ'galɔ]

| shop assistant (masc.) | commesso (m) | [kɔm'mɛssɔ] |
| shop assistant (fem.) | commessa (f) | [kɔm'mɛssa] |

cash desk	cassa (f)	['kassa]
mirror	specchio (m)	['spɛkkiɔ]
counter (in shop)	banco (m)	['baŋkɔ]

fitting room	camerino (m)	[kamɛ'rino]
to try on	provare (vt)	[pro'varɛ]
to fit (ab. dress, etc.)	stare bene	['starɛ 'bɛnɛ]
to fancy (vt)	piacere (vi)	[pja'tʃerɛ]

price	prezzo (m)	['prɛtso]
price tag	etichetta (f) del prezzo	[ɛti'ketta deʎ 'prɛtso]
to cost (vt)	costare (vt)	[kos'tarɛ]
How much?	Quanto?	[ku'anto]
discount	sconto (m)	['skonto]

inexpensive (adj)	no muy caro	[no muj 'karo]
cheap (adj)	a buon mercato	[a bu'on mɛr'kato]
expensive (adj)	caro	['karo]
It's expensive	È caro	[ɛ 'karo]

hire (n)	noleggio (m)	[no'ledʒo]
to hire (~ a dinner jacket)	noleggiare (vt)	[nole'dʒarɛ]
credit	credito (m)	['krɛdito]
on credit (adv)	a credito	[a 'krɛdito]

CLOTHING & ACCESSORIES

32. Outerwear. Coats

clothes	vestiti (m pl)	[vɛs'titi]
outer clothing	soprabito (m)	[sɔp'rabitɔ]
winter clothing	abiti (m pl) invernali	['abiti invɛr'nali]
overcoat	cappotto (m)	[kap'pɔttɔ]
fur coat	pelliccia (f)	[pɛl'litʃa]
fur jacket	pellicciotto (m)	[pɛlli'tʃɔttɔ]
down coat	piumino (m)	[pjy'minɔ]
jacket (e.g. leather ~)	giubbotto (m), giaccha (f)	[dʒub'bɔttɔ], ['dʒakka]
raincoat	impermeabile (m)	[impɛrmɛ'abile]
waterproof (adj)	impermeabile	[impɛrmɛ'abile]

33. Men's & women's clothing

shirt	camicia (f)	[ka'mitʃa]
trousers	pantaloni (m pl)	[panta'lɔni]
jeans	jeans (m pl)	['dʒins]
jacket (of man's suit)	giacca (f)	['dʒakka]
suit	abito (m) da uomo	['abitɔ da u'ɔmɔ]
dress (frock)	abito (m)	['abitɔ]
skirt	gonna (f)	['gɔŋa]
blouse	camicetta (f)	[kami'tʃetta]
knitted jacket	giacca (f) a maglia	['dʒakka a 'maʎja]
jacket (of woman's suit)	giacca (f) tailleur	['dʒaka ta'jer]
T-shirt	maglietta (f)	[ma'ʎjetta]
shorts (short trousers)	pantaloni (m pl) corti	[panta'lɔni 'kɔrti]
tracksuit	tuta (f) sportiva	['tuta spɔr'tiva]
bathrobe	accappatoio (m)	[akkappa'tɔjo]
pyjamas	pigiama (m)	[pi'dʒama]
sweater	maglione (m)	[ma'ʎɔnɛ]
pullover	pullover (m)	[pul'lɔvɛr]
waistcoat	gilè (m)	[dʒi'le]
tailcoat	frac (m)	[frak]
dinner suit	smoking (m)	['zmɔkiŋ]
uniform	uniforme (f)	[uni'fɔrmɛ]
workwear	tuta (f) da lavoro	['tuta da ʎa'vɔrɔ]
boiler suit	salopette (f)	[salɔ'pɛtt]
coat (e.g. doctor's ~)	camice (m)	[ka'mitʃe]

34. Clothing. Underwear

underwear	biancheria (f) intima	[bjaŋkɛ'ria 'intima]
vest (singlet)	maglietta (f) intima	[mali'ɛtta 'intima]
socks	calzini (m pl)	[kaʎ'ʦini]
nightgown	camicia (f) da notte	[ka'miʧa da 'nɔttɛ]
bra	reggiseno (m)	[rɛʤi'sɛnɔ]
knee highs	calzini (m pl) alti	[kaʎ'ʦini 'alti]
tights	collant (m)	[kɔ'ʎant]
stockings	calze (f pl)	['kaʎʦe]
swimsuit, bikini	costume (m) da bagno	[kɔs'tumɛ da 'baɲɔ]

35. Headwear

hat	cappello (m)	[kap'pɛllɔ]
trilby hat	cappello (m) di feltro	[kap'pɛllɔ di feltrɔ]
baseball cap	cappello (m) da baseball	[kap'pɛllɔ da 'bɛjzbɔʎ]
flatcap	coppola (f)	['kɔppɔla]
beret	basco (m)	['baskɔ]
hood	cappuccio (m)	[kap'puʧɔ]
panama	panama (m)	['panama]
knitted hat	berretto (m) a maglia	[bɛr'rɛttɔ a 'maʎja]
headscarf	fazzoletto (m) da capo	[faʦɔ'lettɔ da 'kapɔ]
women's hat	cappellino (m) donna	[kappɛl'linɔ 'dɔɲa]
hard hat	casco (m)	['kaskɔ]
forage cap	bustina (f)	[bus'tina]
helmet	casco (m)	['kaskɔ]
bowler	bombetta (f)	[bɔm'bɛtta]
top hat	cilindro (m)	[ʧi'lindrɔ]

36. Footwear

footwear	calzature (f pl)	[kaʎʦa'turɛ]
ankle boots	stivaletti (m pl)	[stiva'letti]
shoes (low-heeled ~)	scarpe (f pl)	['skarpɛ]
boots (cowboy ~)	stivali (m pl)	[sti'vali]
slippers	pantofole (f pl)	[pan'tofole]
trainers	scarpe (f pl) da tennis	['skarpɛ da 'tɛɲis]
plimsolls, pumps	scarpe (f pl) da ginnastica	['skarpɛ da ʤim'nastika]
sandals	sandali (m pl)	['sandali]
cobbler	calzolaio (m)	[kaʎʦo'ʎajo]
heel	tacco (m)	['takkɔ]
pair (of shoes)	paio (m)	['pajo]
shoelace	laccio (m)	['ʎaʧɔ]

to lace up (vt)	allacciare (vt)	[aʎa'ʧarɛ]
shoehorn	calzascarpe (m)	[kaʎtsas'karpɛ]
shoe polish	lucido (m) per le scarpe	['lytʃidɔ pɛr le 'skarpɛ]

37. Personal accessories

gloves	guanti (m pl)	[gu'anti]
mittens	manopole (f pl)	[ma'nɔpɔle]
scarf (long)	sciarpa (f)	['ʃarpa]

glasses	occhiali (m pl)	[ɔk'kjali]
frame (eyeglass ~)	montatura (f)	[mɔnta'tura]
umbrella	ombrello (m)	[ɔmb'rɛllɔ]
walking stick	bastone (m)	[bas'tɔnɛ]
hairbrush	spazzola (f) per capelli	['spatsɔʎa pɛr ka'pɛlli]
fan	ventaglio (m)	[vɛn'taʎɔ]

tie (necktie)	cravatta (f)	[kra'vatta]
bow tie	cravatta (f) a farfalla	[kra'vatta a far'faʎa]
braces	bretelle (f pl)	[brɛ'tɛlle]
handkerchief	fazzoletto (m)	[fatsɔ'lettɔ]

comb	pettine (m)	['pɛttinɛ]
hair slide	fermaglio (m)	[fɛr'maʎɔ]
hairpin	forcina (f)	[fɔr'ʧina]
buckle	fibbia (f)	['fibbja]

| belt | cintura (f) | [ʧin'tura] |
| shoulder strap | spallina (f) | [spal'lina] |

bag (handbag)	borsa (f)	['bɔrsa]
handbag	borsetta (f)	[bɔr'sɛtta]
rucksack	zaino (m)	['dzainɔ]

38. Clothing. Miscellaneous

fashion	moda (f)	['mɔda]
in vogue (adj)	di moda	[di 'mɔda]
fashion designer	stilista (m)	[sti'lista]

collar	collo (m)	['kɔllɔ]
pocket	tasca (f)	['taska]
pocket (as adj)	tascabile	[tas'kabile]
sleeve	manica (f)	['manika]
hanging loop	asola (f) per appendere	['azɔʎa per ap'pendɛrɛ]
flies (on trousers)	patta (f)	['patta]

zip (fastener)	cerniera (f) lampo	[ʧer'njera 'lampɔ]
fastener	chiusura (f)	[kjy'zura]
button	bottone (m)	[bɔt'tɔnɛ]
buttonhole	occhiello (m)	[ɔk'kjellɔ]
to come off (ab. button)	staccarsi (vr)	[stak'karsi]

to sew (vi, vt)	cucire (vi, vt)	[ku'ʧirɛ]
to embroider (vi, vt)	ricamare (vi, vt)	[rika'marɛ]
embroidery	ricamo (m)	[ri'kamɔ]
sewing needle	ago (m)	['agɔ]
thread	filo (m)	['filɔ]
seam	cucitura (f)	[kuʧi'tura]

to get dirty (vi)	sporcarsi (vr)	[spɔr'karsi]
stain (mark, spot)	macchia (f)	['makkja]
to crease, crumple (vi)	sgualcirsi (vr)	[zguaʎ'ʧirsi]
to tear (vt)	strappare (vt)	[strap'parɛ]
clothes moth	tarma (f)	['tarma]

39. Personal care. Cosmetics

toothpaste	dentifricio (m)	[dɛntif'riʧɔ]
toothbrush	spazzolino (m) da denti	[spaʦo'lino da 'dɛnti]
to clean one's teeth	lavarsi i denti	[ʎa'varsi i 'dɛnti]

razor	rasoio (m)	[ra'zɔjo]
shaving cream	crema (f) da barba	['krɛma da 'barba]
to shave (vi)	rasarsi (vr)	[ra'zarsi]

soap	sapone (m)	[sa'ponɛ]
shampoo	shampoo (m)	['ʃampɔ]

scissors	forbici (f pl)	['forbiʧi]
nail file	limetta (f)	[li'mɛtta]
nail clippers	tagliaunghie (m)	[taʎa'ungje]
tweezers	pinzette (f pl)	[pin'ʦɛttɛ]

cosmetics	cosmetica (f)	[kɔz'mɛtika]
face pack	maschera (f) di bellezza	['maskɛra di bɛl'leʦa]
manicure	manicure (m)	[mani'kyrɛ]
to have a manicure	fare la manicure	['farɛ ʎa mani'kurɛ]
pedicure	pedicure (m)	[pɛdi'kyrɛ]

make-up bag	borsa (f) del trucco	['bɔrsa dɛʎ 'trukkɔ]
face powder	cipria (f)	['ʧipria]
powder compact	portacipria (m)	[pɔrta'ʧipria]
blusher	fard (m)	[far]

perfume (bottled)	profumo (m)	[prɔ'fumɔ]
toilet water	acqua (f) da toeletta	['akva da tɔɛ'lɛtta]
lotion	lozione (f)	[lɔ'ʦjonɛ]
cologne	acqua (f) di Colonia	['akua di kɔ'lɔɲa]

eyeshadow	ombretto (m)	[ɔmb'rɛttɔ]
eyeliner	eyeliner (m)	[aj'lajnɛr]
mascara	mascara (m)	[mas'kara]

lipstick	rossetto (m)	[rɔs'sɛttɔ]
nail polish	smalto (m)	['zmaʎtɔ]
hair spray	lacca (f) per capelli	['ʎakka per ka'pɛlli]

deodorant	**deodorante** (m)	[dɛodo'rantɛ]
cream	**crema** (f)	['krɛma]
face cream	**crema** (f) **per il viso**	['krɛma pɛr iʎ 'wizɔ]
hand cream	**crema** (f) **per le mani**	['krɛma pɛr le 'mani]
anti-wrinkle cream	**crema** (f) **antirughe**	['krɛma anti'rugɛ]
day (as adj)	**da giorno**	[da 'dʒɔrnɔ]
night (as adj)	**da notte**	[da 'nɔttɛ]
tampon	**tampone** (m)	[tam'pɔnɛ]
toilet paper	**carta** (f) **igienica**	['karta i'dʒenika]
hair dryer	**fon** (m)	[fɔn]

40. Watches. Clocks

watch (wristwatch)	**orologio** (m)	[ɔrɔ'lɔdʒɔ]
dial	**quadrante** (m)	[kuad'rantɛ]
hand (of clock, watch)	**lancetta** (f)	[ʎan'ʧetta]
metal bracelet	**braccialetto** (m)	[braʧa'lettɔ]
watch strap	**cinturino** (m)	[ʧintu'rinɔ]
battery	**pila** (f)	['piʎa]
to be flat (battery)	**essere scarico**	['ɛssɛrɛ 'skarikɔ]
to change a battery	**cambiare la pila**	[kam'bjarɛ ʎa 'piʎa]
to run fast	**andare avanti**	[an'darɛ a'vanti]
to run slow	**andare indietro**	[an'darɛ indri'etrɔ]
wall clock	**orologio** (m) **da muro**	[ɔrɔ'lɔdʒɔ da 'murɔ]
hourglass	**clessidra** (f)	['klessidra]
sundial	**orologio** (m) **solare**	[ɔrɔ'lɔdʒɔ sɔ'ʎarɛ]
alarm clock	**sveglia** (f)	['zvɛʎja]
watchmaker	**orologiaio** (m)	[ɔrɔlɔ'dʒajo]
to repair (vt)	**riparare** (vt)	[ripa'rarɛ]

EVERYDAY EXPERIENCE

41. Money

money	**soldi** (m pl)	['soʎdi]
exchange	**cambio** (m)	['kambjo]
exchange rate	**corso** (m) **di cambio**	['korso di 'kambjo]
cashpoint	**bancomat** (m)	['baŋkomat]
coin	**moneta** (f)	[mo'nɛta]
dollar	**dollaro** (m)	['doʎaro]
euro	**euro** (m)	['ɛuro]
lira	**lira** (f)	['lira]
Deutschmark	**marco** (m)	['marko]
franc	**franco** (m)	['fraŋko]
pound sterling	**sterlina** (f)	[stɛr'lina]
yen	**yen** (m)	[jen]
debt	**debito** (m)	['dɛbito]
debtor	**debitore** (m)	[dɛbi'torɛ]
to lend (money)	**prestare** (vt)	[pres'tarɛ]
to borrow (vi, vt)	**prendere in prestito**	['prɛndɛrɛ in 'prɛstito]
bank	**banca** (f)	['baŋka]
account	**conto** (m)	['konto]
to deposit into the account	**versare sul conto**	[vɛr'sarɛ suʎ 'konto]
to withdraw (vt)	**prelevare dal conto**	[prɛle'varɛ daʎ 'konto]
credit card	**carta** (f) **di credito**	['karta di 'krɛdito]
cash	**contanti** (m pl)	[kon'tanti]
cheque	**assegno** (m)	[as'sɛɲo]
to write a cheque	**emettere un assegno**	[ɛ'mɛttɛrɛ un as'sɛɲo]
chequebook	**libretto** (m) **di assegni**	[lib'rɛtto di as'sɛɲi]
wallet	**portafoglio** (m)	[porta'foʎo]
purse	**borsellino** (m)	[borsɛl'lino]
billfold	**portamonete** (m)	[portamo'nɛtɛ]
safe	**cassaforte** (f)	[kassa'fortɛ]
heir	**erede** (m)	[ɛ'rɛdɛ]
inheritance	**eredità** (f)	[ɛrɛdi'ta]
fortune (wealth)	**fortuna** (f)	[for'tuna]
lease, let	**affitto** (m)	[af'fitto]
rent money	**affitto** (m)	[af'fitto]
to rent (sth from sb)	**affittare** (vt)	[affit'tarɛ]
price	**prezzo** (m)	['prɛtso]
cost	**costo** (m), **prezzo** (m)	['kosto], ['prɛtso]

sum	somma (f)	['sɔmma]
to spend (vt)	spendere (vt)	['spɛndɛrɛ]
expenses	spese (f pl)	['spɛzɛ]
to economize (vi, vt)	economizzare (vi, vt)	[ɛkɔnɔmi'dzarɛ]
thrifty (adj)	economico	[ɛkɔ'nɔmikɔ]

to pay (vi, vt)	pagare (vi, vt)	[pa'garɛ]
payment	pagamento (m)	[paga'mɛntɔ]
change (give the ~)	resto (m)	['rɛstɔ]

tax	imposta (f)	[im'pɔsta]
fine	multa (f), ammenda (f)	['muʎta], [am'mɛnda]
to fine (vt)	multare (vt)	[muʎ'tarɛ]

42. Post. Postal service

post office	posta (f), ufficio (m) postale	['pɔsta], [uf'fitʃɔ pɔs'tale]
post (letters, etc.)	posta (f)	['pɔsta]
postman	postino (m)	[pɔs'tinɔ]
opening hours	orario (m) di apertura	[ɔ'rariɔ di apɛr'tura]

letter	lettera (f)	['lettɛra]
registered letter	raccomandata (f)	[rakkɔman'data]
postcard	cartolina (f)	[kartɔ'lina]
telegram	telegramma (m)	[tɛleg'ramma]
parcel	pacco (m) postale	['pakkɔ pɔs'tale]
money transfer	vaglia (m) postale	['vaʎja pɔs'tale]

to receive (vt)	ricevere (vt)	[ri'tʃevɛrɛ]
to send (vt)	spedire (vt)	[spɛ'dirɛ]
sending	invio (m)	[in'wiɔ]

address	indirizzo (m)	[indi'ritsɔ]
postcode	codice (m) postale	['kɔditʃe pɔs'tale]
sender	mittente (m)	[mit'tɛntɛ]
receiver, addressee	destinatario (m)	[dɛstina'tariɔ]
name	nome (m)	['nɔmɛ]
family name	cognome (m)	[kɔ'ɲɔmɛ]

rate (of postage)	tariffa (f)	[ta'riffa]
standard (adj)	ordinario	[ɔrdi'nariɔ]
economical (adj)	standard	['standar]

weight	peso (m)	['pɛzɔ]
to weigh up (vt)	pesare (vt)	[pɛ'zarɛ]
envelope	busta (f)	['busta]
postage stamp	francobollo (m)	[frankɔ'bɔllɔ]

43. Banking

bank	banca (f)	['banka]
branch (of bank, etc.)	filiale (f)	[fili'ale]

consultant	consulente (m)	[kɔnsu'lentɛ]
manager (director)	direttore (m)	[diret'tɔrɛ]

bank account	conto (m) bancario	['kɔntɔ ba'ŋkariɔ]
account number	numero (m) del conto	['numɛrɔ dɛʎ 'kɔntɔ]
current account	conto (m) corrente	['kɔntɔ kɔr'rɛntɛ]
deposit account	conto (m) di risparmio	['kɔntɔ di ris'parmiɔ]

to open an account	aprire un conto	[ap'rirɛ un 'kɔntɔ]
to close the account	chiudere il conto	['kjydɛrɛ iʎ 'kɔntɔ]
to deposit into the account	versare sul conto	[vɛr'sare suʎ 'kɔntɔ]
to withdraw (vt)	prelevare dal conto	[prɛle'varɛ daʎ 'kɔntɔ]

deposit	deposito (m)	[dɛ'pozitɔ]
to make a deposit	depositare (vt)	[dɛpozi'tarɛ]
wire transfer	trasferimento (m) telegrafico	[trasfɛri'mɛntɔ tɛleg'rafikɔ]
to wire (money)	rimettere i soldi	[ri'mɛttɛrɛ i 'sɔʎdi]

sum	somma (f)	['sɔmma]
How much?	Quanto?	[ku'antɔ]

signature	firma (f)	['firma]
to sign (vt)	firmare (vt)	[fir'marɛ]

credit card	carta (f) di credito	['karta di 'krɛditɔ]
code	codice (m)	['kɔditʃe]
credit card number	numero (m) della carta di credito	['numɛrɔ 'dɛʎa 'karta di 'krɛditɔ]

cashpoint	bancomat (m)	['baŋkɔmat]

cheque	assegno (m)	[as'sɛɲɔ]
to write a cheque	emettere un assegno	[ɛ'mɛttɛrɛ un as'sɛɲɔ]
chequebook	libretto (m) di assegni	[lib'rɛttɔ di as'sɛɲi]

loan (bank ~)	prestito (m)	['prɛstitɔ]
to apply for a loan	fare domanda per un prestito	['farɛ dɔ'manda pɛr un 'prɛstitɔ]
to get a loan	ottenere un prestito	[ɔttɛ'nɛrɛ un 'prɛstitɔ]
to give a loan	concedere un prestito	[kɔn'tʃedɛrɛ un 'prɛstitɔ]
guarantee	garanzia (f)	[garan'tsia]

44. Telephone. Phone conversation

telephone	telefono (m)	[tɛ'lefɔnɔ]
mobile phone	telefonino (m)	[tɛlefɔ'ninɔ]
answering machine	segreteria (f) telefonica	[sɛgrɛtɛ'ria tɛle'fɔnika]

to ring (telephone)	telefonare (vi, vt)	[tɛlefɔ'narɛ]
call, ring	chiamata (f)	[kja'mata]

to dial a number	comporre un numero	[kɔm'pɔrrɛ un 'numɛrɔ]
Hello!	Pronto!	['prontɔ]
to ask (vt)	chiedere, domandare	['kjedɛrɛ], [dɔman'darɛ]
to answer (vi, vt)	rispondere (vi, vt)	[ris'pɔndɛrɛ]

to hear (vt)	udire, sentire (vt)	[u'dirɛ], [sɛn'tirɛ]
well (adv)	bene	['bɛnɛ]
not well (adv)	male	['male]
noises (interference)	disturbi (m pl)	[dis'turbi]

receiver	cornetta (f)	[kɔr'nɛtta]
to pick up (~ the phone)	alzare la cornetta	[aʎ'tsarɛ ʎa kɔr'nɛtta]
to hang up (~ the phone)	riattaccare la cornetta	[riattak'karɛ ʎa kɔr'nɛtta]

engaged (adj)	occupato	[ɔkku'patɔ]
to ring (ab. phone)	squillare (vi)	[skui'ʎarɛ]
telephone book	elenco (m) telefonico	[ɛ'leŋkɔ tɛle'fɔnikɔ]

local (adj)	locale	[lɜ'kale]
trunk (e.g. ~ call)	interurbano	[intɛrur'banɔ]
international (adj)	internazionale	[intɛrnatsʲɔ'nale]

45. Mobile telephone

mobile phone	telefonino (m)	[tɛlefɔ'ninɔ]
display	schermo (m)	['skɛrmɔ]
button	tasto (m)	['tastɔ]
SIM card	scheda SIM (f)	['skɛda 'sim]

battery	pila (f)	['piʎa]
to be flat (battery)	essere scarico	['ɛssɛrɛ 'skarikɔ]
charger	caricabatteria (m)	[karikabattɛ'ria]

menu	menù (m)	[me'nu]
settings	impostazioni (f pl)	[impɔsta'tsʲɔni]
tune (melody)	melodia (f)	[mɛlɜ'dia]
to select (vt)	scegliere (vt)	['ʃeʎjerɛ]

calculator	calcolatrice (f)	[kaʎkɔʎat'ritʃe]
answering machine	segreteria (f) telefonica	[sɛgrɛtɛ'ria tɛle'fɔnika]
alarm clock	sveglia (f)	['zvɛʎja]
contacts	contatti (m pl)	[kɔn'tatti]

| SMS (text message) | messaggio (m) SMS | [mes'sadʒɔ ɛsɛ'mɛsɛ] |
| subscriber | abbonato (m) | [abbɔ'natɔ] |

46. Stationery

| ballpoint pen | penna (f) a sfera | [peŋa a 'sfɛra] |
| fountain pen | penna (f) stilografica | ['pɛŋa stilɔg'rafika] |

pencil	matita (f)	[ma'tita]
highlighter	evidenziatore (m)	[ɛwidɛntsja'tɔrɛ]
felt-tip pen	pennarello (m)	[peŋa'rɛllɔ]

| notepad | taccuino (m) | [takku'inɔ] |
| diary | agenda (f) | [a'dʒɛnda] |

ruler	**righello** (m)	[ri'gɛllɔ]
calculator	**calcolatrice** (f)	[kaʎkoʎat'ritʃe]
rubber	**gomma** (f) **per cancellare**	['gɔmma pɛr kantʃe'ʎarɛ]
drawing pin	**puntina** (f)	[pun'tina]
paper clip	**graffetta** (f)	[graf'fɛtta]

glue	**colla** (f)	['kɔʎa]
stapler	**pinzatrice** (f)	[pintsat'ritʃe]
hole punch	**perforatrice** (f)	[pɛrforat'ritʃɛ]
pencil sharpener	**temperamatite** (m)	[tɛmpɛrama'titɛ]

47. Foreign languages

language	**lingua** (f)	['liŋua]
foreign (adj)	**straniero**	[stra'njerɔ]
to study (vt)	**studiare** (vt)	[studi'arɛ]
to learn (language, etc.)	**imparare** (vt)	[impa'rarɛ]

to read (vi, vt)	**leggere** (vi, vt)	['ledʒerɛ]
to speak (vi, vt)	**parlare** (vi, vt)	[par'ʎarɛ]
to understand (vt)	**capire** (vt)	[ka'pirɛ]
to write (vt)	**scrivere** (vi, vt)	['skrivɛrɛ]

fast (adv)	**rapidamente**	[rapida'mɛntɛ]
slowly (adv)	**lentamente**	[lenta'mɛntɛ]
fluently (adv)	**correntemente**	[kɔrrɛntɛ'mɛntɛ]

rules	**regole** (f pl)	['rɛgole]
grammar	**grammatica** (f)	[gram'matika]
vocabulary	**lessico** (m)	['lessikɔ]
phonetics	**fonetica** (f)	[fɔ'nɛtika]

textbook	**manuale** (m)	[manu'ale]
dictionary	**dizionario** (m)	[ditsɔ'nariɔ]
teach-yourself book	**manuale** (m) **autodidattico**	[manu'ale autɔdi'dattikɔ]
phrasebook	**frasario** (m)	[fra'zariɔ]

cassette	**cassetta** (f)	[kas'sɛtta]
videotape	**videocassetta** (f)	[widɛɔkas'sɛtta]
CD, compact disc	**CD** (m)	[tʃi'di]
DVD	**DVD** (m)	[divu'di]

alphabet	**alfabeto** (m)	[aʎfa'bɛtɔ]
to spell (vt)	**compitare** (vt)	[kɔmpi'tarɛ]
pronunciation	**pronuncia** (f)	[prɔ'nuntʃa]

accent	**accento** (m)	[a'tʃentɔ]
with an accent	**con un accento**	[kɔn un a'tʃentɔ]
without an accent	**senza accento**	['sɛntsa a'tʃentɔ]

word	**vocabolo** (m)	[vɔ'kabɔlɔ]
meaning	**significato** (m)	[siŋ'ifi'katɔ]
course (e.g. a French ~)	**corso** (m)	['kɔrsɔ]
to sign up	**iscriversi** (vr)	[isk'rivɛrsi]

teacher	insegnante (m, f)	[insɛ'ɲjantɛ]
translation (process)	traduzione (f)	[tradu'tsjonɛ]
translation (text, etc.)	traduzione (f)	[tradu'tsjonɛ]
translator	traduttore (m)	[tradut'torɛ]
interpreter	interprete (m)	[in'tɛrprɛtɛ]
polyglot	poliglotta (m)	[polig'lɔtta]
memory	memoria (f)	[mɛ'mɔria]

MEALS. RESTAURANT

48. Table setting

spoon	cucchiaio (m)	[kuk'kjajo]
knife	coltello (m)	[koʎ'tɛllɔ]
fork	forchetta (f)	[for'kɛtta]
cup (of coffee)	tazza (f)	['tatʦa]
plate (dinner ~)	piatto (m)	['pjattɔ]
saucer	piattino (m)	[pjat'tinɔ]
serviette	tovagliolo (m)	[tɔva'ʎiɔlɔ]
toothpick	stuzzicadenti (m)	[stutʦika'dɛnti]

49. Restaurant

restaurant	ristorante (m)	[risto'rantɛ]
coffee bar	caffè (m)	[kaf'fɛ]
pub, bar	pub (m), bar (m)	[pab], [bar]
tearoom	sala (f) da tè	['saʎa da 'tɛ]
waiter	cameriere (m)	[kamɛ'rjerɛ]
waitress	cameriera (f)	[kamɛ'rjera]
barman	barista (m)	[ba'rista]
menu	menù (m)	[me'nu]
wine list	carta (f) dei vini	['karta dɛi 'wini]
to book a table	prenotare un tavolo	[prɛnɔ'tarɛ un 'tavɔlɔ]
course, dish	piatto (m)	['pjattɔ]
to order (meal)	ordinare (vt)	[ordi'narɛ]
to make an order	fare un'ordinazione	['farɛ unordina'ʦionɛ]
aperitif	aperitivo (m)	[apɛri'tivo]
starter	antipasto (m)	[anti'pastɔ]
dessert, sweet	dolce (m)	['dɔʎtʃe]
bill	conto (m)	['kɔntɔ]
to pay the bill	pagare il conto	[pa'garɛ iʎ 'kɔntɔ]
to give change	dare il resto	['darɛ iʎ 'rɛstɔ]
tip	mancia (f)	['mantʃa]

50. Meals

food	cibo (m)	['tʃibɔ]
to eat (vi, vt)	mangiare (vi, vt)	[man'dʒarɛ]

breakfast	colazione (f)	[koʎa'tsione]
to have breakfast	fare colazione	['farɛ koʎa'tsione]
lunch	pranzo (m)	['prantso]
to have lunch	pranzare (vi)	[pran'tsarɛ]
dinner	cena (f)	['tʃena]
to have dinner	cenare (vi)	[tʃe'narɛ]

| appetite | appetito (m) | [appɛ'tito] |
| Enjoy your meal! | Buon appetito! | [bu'ɔn appɛ'tito] |

to open (~ a bottle)	aprire (vt)	[ap'rirɛ]
to spill (liquid)	rovesciare (vt)	[rɔve'ʃarɛ]
to spill out (vi)	rovesciarsi (vi)	[rɔve'ʃarsi]

to boil (vi)	bollire (vi)	[bɔl'lirɛ]
to boil (vt)	far bollire	[far bɔl'lirɛ]
boiled (~ water)	bollito	[bɔl'lito]
to cool (vt)	raffreddare (vt)	[raffrɛ'darɛ]
to cool down (vi)	raffreddarsi (vr)	[raffrɛd'darsi]

| taste, flavour | gusto (m) | ['gusto] |
| aftertaste | retrogusto (m) | [rɛtro'gusto] |

to be on a diet	essere a dieta	['ɛssɛrɛ a di'ɛta]
diet	dieta (f)	[di'ɛta]
vitamin	vitamina (f)	[wita'mina]
calorie	caloria (f)	[kalɔ'ria]
vegetarian (n)	vegetariano (m)	[vɛdʒetari'ano]
vegetarian (adj)	vegetariano	[vɛdʒetari'ano]

fats (nutrient)	grassi (m pl)	['grassi]
proteins	proteine (f pl)	[prɔtɛ'inɛ]
carbohydrates	carboidrati (m pl)	[karbɔid'rati]
slice (of lemon, ham)	fetta (f), fettina (f)	['fetta], [fet'tina]
piece (of cake, pie)	pezzo (m)	['pɛtso]
crumb (of bread)	briciola (f)	['britʃoʎa]

51. Cooked dishes

course, dish	piatto (m)	['pjatto]
cuisine	cucina (f)	[ku'tʃina]
recipe	ricetta (f)	[ri'tʃetta]
portion	porzione (f)	[pɔr'tsione]

| salad | insalata (f) | [insa'ʎata] |
| soup | minestra (f) | [mi'nɛstra] |

clear soup (broth)	brodo (m)	['brɔdɔ]
sandwich (bread)	panino (m)	[pa'nino]
fried eggs	uova (f pl) al tegamino	[u'ova aʎ tɛga'minɔ]

cutlet	cotoletta (f)	[kɔtɔ'letta]
hamburger (beefburger)	hamburger (m)	[am'burger]
beefsteak	bistecca (f)	[bis'tɛkka]

roast meat	arrosto (m)	[ar'rɔstɔ]
garnish	contorno (m)	[kɔn'tɔrnɔ]
spaghetti	spaghetti (m pl)	[spa'gɛtti]
mash	purè (m) di patate	[pu'rɛ di pa'tatɛ]
pizza	pizza (f)	['pitsa]
porridge (oatmeal, etc.)	porridge (m)	[pɔr'ridʒɛ]
omelette	frittata (f)	[frit'tata]

boiled (e.g. ~ beef)	bollito	[bɔl'litɔ]
smoked (adj)	affumicato	[affumi'katɔ]
fried (adj)	fritto	['frittɔ]
dried (adj)	secco	['sɛkkɔ]
frozen (adj)	congelato	[kɔndʒe'ʎatɔ]
pickled (adj)	sottaceto	[sottʃa'tʃetɔ]

sweet (sugary)	dolce	['dɔʎtʃe]
salty (adj)	salato	[sa'ʎatɔ]
cold (adj)	freddo	['freddɔ]
hot (adj)	caldo	['kaʎdɔ]
bitter (adj)	amaro	[a'marɔ]
tasty (adj)	buono, gustoso	[bu'ɔnɔ], [gus'tɔzɔ]

to cook (in boiling water)	cuocere, preparare (vt)	[ku'ɔtʃerɛ], [prepa'rarɛ]
to cook (dinner)	cucinare (vi)	[kutʃi'narɛ]
to fry (vt)	friggere (vt)	['fridʒerɛ]
to heat up (food)	riscaldare (vt)	[riskaʎ'darɛ]

to salt (vt)	salare (vt)	[sa'ʎarɛ]
to pepper (vt)	pepare (vt)	[pɛ'parɛ]
to grate (vt)	grattugiare (vt)	[grattu'dʒarɛ]
peel (n)	buccia (f)	['butʃa]
to peel (vt)	sbucciare (vt)	[zbu'tʃarɛ]

52. Food

meat	carne (f)	['karnɛ]
chicken	pollo (m)	['pollɔ]
young chicken	pollo (m) novello	['pollɔ no'vɛllɔ]
duck	anatra (f)	['anatra]
goose	oca (f)	['ɔka]
game	cacciagione (f)	[katʃa'dʒɔnɛ]
turkey	tacchino (m)	[tak'kinɔ]

pork	carne (m) di maiale	['karnɛ di ma'jale]
veal	vitello (m)	[wi'tɛllɔ]
lamb	carne (f) di agnello	['karnɛ di a'nɛllɔ]
beef	manzo (m)	['mandzɔ]
rabbit	coniglio (m)	[kɔ'niʎɔ]

sausage (salami, etc.)	salame (m)	[sa'ʎamɛ]
vienna sausage	wüsterl (m)	['wy:stɛrʎ]
bacon	pancetta (f)	[pan'tʃetta]
ham	prosciutto (m)	[prɔ'ʃuttɔ]
gammon (ham)	prosciutto (m) affumicato	[prɔ'ʃuttɔ affumi'katɔ]

pâté	**pâté** (m)	[pa'tɛ]
liver	**fegato** (m)	['fɛgatɔ]
lard	**lardo** (m)	['ʎardɔ]
mince	**carne** (f) **trita**	['karnɛ 'trita]
tongue	**lingua** (f)	['liɲua]
egg	**uovo** (m)	[u'ovɔ]
eggs	**uova** (f pl)	[u'ova]
egg white	**albume** (m)	[aʎ'bumɛ]
egg yolk	**tuorlo** (m)	[tu'ɔrlɔ]
fish	**pesce** (m)	['pɛʃɛ]
seafood	**frutti** (m pl) **di mare**	['frutti di 'marɛ]
crustaceans	**crostacei** (m pl)	[krɔs'tatʃei]
caviar	**caviale** (m)	[ka'vjale]
crab	**granchio** (m)	['graɲkiɔ]
prawn	**gamberetto** (m)	[gambɛ'rɛttɔ]
oyster	**ostrica** (f)	['ɔstrika]
spiny lobster	**aragosta** (f)	[ara'gɔsta]
octopus	**polpo** (m)	['pɔʎpɔ]
squid	**calamaro** (m)	[kaʎa'marɔ]
sturgeon	**storione** (m)	[stori'ɔnɛ]
salmon	**salmone** (m)	[saʎ'monɛ]
halibut	**ippoglosso** (m)	[ippɔg'lɔssɔ]
cod	**merluzzo** (m)	[mɛr'lytsɔ]
mackerel	**scombro** (m)	['skɔmbrɔ]
tuna	**tonno** (m)	['tɔnɔ]
eel	**anguilla** (f)	[aɲu'iʎa]
trout	**trota** (f)	['trɔta]
sardine	**sardina** (f)	[sar'dina]
pike	**luccio** (m)	['lytʃɔ]
herring	**aringa** (f)	[a'riɲa]
bread	**pane** (m)	['panɛ]
cheese	**formaggio** (m)	[fɔr'madʒɔ]
sugar	**zucchero** (m)	['dzukkɛrɔ]
salt	**sale** (m)	['sale]
rice	**riso** (m)	['rizɔ]
pasta	**pasta** (f)	['pasta]
noodles	**tagliatelle** (f pl)	[taʎja'tɛlle]
butter	**burro** (m)	['burrɔ]
vegetable oil	**olio** (m) **vegetale**	['ɔʎɔ wedʒe'tale]
sunflower oil	**olio** (m) **di girasole**	['ɔʎɔ di dʒira'sole]
margarine	**margarina** (f)	[marga'rina]
olives	**olive** (f pl)	[ɔ'livɛ]
olive oil	**olio** (m) **d'oliva**	['ɔʎɔ dɔ'liva]
milk	**latte** (m)	['ʎattɛ]
condensed milk	**latte** (m) **condensato**	['ʎattɛ kɔndɛn'satɔ]

yogurt	yogurt (m)	['jogurt]
sour cream	panna (f) acida	['paɲa 'atʃida]
cream (of milk)	panna (f)	['paɲa]

| mayonnaise | maionese (m) | [majo'nɛzɛ] |
| buttercream | crema (f) | ['krɛma] |

groats	cereali (m pl)	[tʃerɛ'ali]
flour	farina (f)	[fa'rina]
tinned food	cibi (m pl) in scatola	['tʃibi in 'skatɔla]

cornflakes	fiocchi (m pl) di mais	['fɔkki di 'mais]
honey	miele (m)	['mjele]
jam	marmellata (f)	[marmɛ'ʎata]
chewing gum	gomma (f) da masticare	['gɔmma da masti'karɛ]

53. Drinks

water	acqua (f)	['akua]
drinking water	acqua (f) potabile	['akua po'tabile]
mineral water	acqua (f) minerale	['akua mine'rale]

still (adj)	liscia, non gassata	['liʃa], [nɔn gas'sata]
carbonated (adj)	gassata	[gas'sata]
sparkling (adj)	frizzante	[fri'dzantɛ]
ice	ghiaccio (m)	['gjatʃɔ]
with ice	con ghiaccio	[kɔn 'gjatʃɔ]

non-alcoholic (adj)	analcolico	[anaʎ'kɔlikɔ]
soft drink	bevanda (f) analcolica	[bɛ'vanda anaʎ'kɔlika]
cool soft drink	bibita (f)	['bibita]
lemonade	limonata (f)	[limɔ'nata]

spirits	bevande (f pl) alcoliche	[bɛ'vandɛ aʎ'kɔlikɛ]
wine	vino (m)	['winɔ]
white wine	vino (m) bianco	['winɔ 'bjaŋkɔ]
red wine	vino (m) rosso	['winɔ 'rɔssɔ]

liqueur	liquore (m)	[liku'ɔrɛ]
champagne	champagne (m)	[ʃam'paɲ]
vermouth	vermouth (m)	['vɛrmut]

whisky	whisky	[u'iski]
vodka	vodka (f)	['vɔdka]
gin	gin (m)	[dʒin]
cognac	cognac (m)	['kɔɲjak]
rum	rum (m)	[rum]

coffee	caffè (m)	[kaf'fɛ]
black coffee	caffè (m) nero	[kaf'fɛ 'nɛrɔ]
white coffee	caffè latte (m)	[kaf'fɛ 'lattɛ]
cappuccino	cappuccino (m)	[kappu'tʃinɔ]
instant coffee	caffè (m) solubile	[kaf'fɛ sɔ'lybile]
milk	latte (m)	['ʎattɛ]

| cocktail | cocktail (m) | [ˈkɔktɛjʎ] |
| milk shake | frullato (m) | [frulˈlato] |

juice	succo (m)	[ˈsukkɔ]
tomato juice	succo (m) di pomodoro	[ˈsukkɔ di pɔmoˈdɔrɔ]
orange juice	succo (m) d'arancia	[ˈsukkɔ daˈrantʃa]
freshly squeezed juice	spremuta (f)	[sprɛˈmuta]

beer	birra (f)	[ˈbirra]
lager	birra (f) chiara	[ˈbirra ˈkjara]
bitter	birra (f) scura	[ˈbirra ˈskura]

tea	tè (m)	[tɛ]
black tea	tè (m) nero	[tɛ ˈnɛrɔ]
green tea	tè (m) verde	[tɛ ˈvɛrdɛ]

54. Vegetables

| vegetables | ortaggi (m pl) | [ɔrˈtadʒi] |
| greens | verdura (f) | [vɛrˈdura] |

tomato	pomodoro (m)	[pɔmoˈdɔrɔ]
cucumber	cetriolo (m)	[tʃetriˈɔlɔ]
carrot	carota (f)	[kaˈrɔta]
potato	patata (f)	[paˈtata]
onion	cipolla (f)	[tʃiˈpoʎa]
garlic	aglio (m)	[ˈaʎɔ]

cabbage	cavolo (m)	[ˈkavɔlɔ]
cauliflower	cavolfiore (m)	[kavɔʎˈfjorɛ]
Brussels sprouts	cavoletti (m pl) di Bruxelles	[kavɔˈletti di brukˈsɛʎ]
broccoli	broccolo (m)	[ˈbrɔkkɔlɔ]

beetroot	barbabietola (f)	[barbaˈbjetɔʎa]
aubergine	melanzana (f)	[mɛʎanˈtsana]
marrow	zucchina (f)	[dzukˈkina]
pumpkin	zucca (f)	[ˈdzukka]
turnip	rapa (f)	[ˈrapa]

parsley	prezzemolo (m)	[prɛˈtsɛmɔlɔ]
dill	aneto (m)	[aˈnɛtɔ]
lettuce	lattuga (f)	[ʎatˈtuga]
celery	sedano (m)	[ˈsɛdanɔ]
asparagus	asparago (m)	[asˈparagɔ]
spinach	spinaci (m pl)	[spiˈnatʃi]

pea	pisello (m)	[piˈzɛllɔ]
beans	fave (f pl)	[ˈfavɛ]
maize	mais (m)	[ˈmais]
kidney bean	fagiolo (m)	[faˈdʒɔlɔ]

bell pepper	peperone (m)	[pepɛˈrɔnɛ]
radish	ravanello (m)	[ravaˈnɛllɔ]
artichoke	carciofo (m)	[karˈtʃɔfɔ]

55. Fruits. Nuts

fruit	**frutto** (m)	['fruttɔ]
apple	**mela** (f)	['mɛʎa]
pear	**pera** (f)	['pɛra]
lemon	**limone** (m)	[li'mɔnɛ]
orange	**arancia** (f)	[a'rantʃa]
strawberry	**fragola** (f)	['fragɔʎa]
tangerine	**mandarino** (m)	[manda'rinɔ]
plum	**prugna** (f)	['pruɲja]
peach	**pesca** (f)	['pɛska]
apricot	**albicocca** (f)	[aʎbi'kɔkka]
raspberry	**lampone** (m)	[ʎam'pɔnɛ]
pineapple	**ananas** (m)	[ana'nas]
banana	**banana** (f)	[ba'nana]
watermelon	**anguria** (f)	[a'ŋuria]
grape	**uva** (f)	['uva]
sour cherry	**amarena** (f)	[ama'rɛna]
sweet cherry	**ciliegia** (f)	[tʃi'ʎjedʒa]
melon	**melone** (m)	[mɛ'lɔnɛ]
grapefruit	**pompelmo** (m)	[pɔm'pɛʎmɔ]
avocado	**avocado** (m)	[avɔ'kadɔ]
papaya	**papaia** (f)	[pa'paja]
mango	**mango** (m)	['maŋɔ]
pomegranate	**melagrana** (f)	[mɛlag'rana]
redcurrant	**ribes** (m) **rosso**	['ribɛs 'rɔssɔ]
blackcurrant	**ribes** (m) **nero**	['ribɛs 'nɛrɔ]
gooseberry	**uva** (f) **spina**	['uva 'spina]
bilberry	**mirtillo** (m)	[mir'tillɔ]
blackberry	**mora** (f)	['mɔra]
raisin	**uvetta** (f)	[u'vɛtta]
fig	**fico** (m)	['fikɔ]
date	**dattero** (m)	['dattɛrɔ]
peanut	**arachide** (f)	[a'rakidɛ]
almond	**mandorla** (f)	['mandɔrʎa]
walnut	**noce** (f)	['nɔtʃe]
hazelnut	**nocciola** (f)	[nɔ'tʃɔʎa]
coconut	**noce** (f) **di cocco**	['nɔtʃe di 'kɔkkɔ]
pistachios	**pistacchi** (m pl)	[pis'takki]

56. Bread. Sweets

confectionery (pastry)	**pasticceria** (f)	[pastitʃe'ria]
bread	**pane** (m)	['panɛ]
biscuits	**biscotti** (m pl)	[bis'kɔtti]
chocolate (n)	**cioccolato** (m)	[tʃɔkkɔ'ʎatɔ]
chocolate (as adj)	**al cioccolato**	[aʎ tʃɔkkɔ'ʎatɔ]

sweet	caramella (f)	[kara'mɛlla]
cake (e.g. cupcake)	tortina (f)	[tɔr'tina]
cake (e.g. birthday ~)	torta (f)	['tɔrta]

| pie (e.g. apple ~) | crostata (f) | [krɔs'tata] |
| filling (for cake, pie) | ripieno (m) | [ri'pjenɔ] |

whole fruit jam	marmellata (f)	[marmɛ'ʎata]
marmalade	marmellata (f) di agrumi	[marmɛ'ʎata di ag'rumi]
waffle	wafer (m)	['vafɛr]
ice-cream	gelato (m)	[dʒe'ʎatɔ]
pudding	budino (m)	[bu'dinɔ]

57. Spices

salt	sale (m)	['sale]
salty (adj)	salato	[sa'ʎatɔ]
to salt (vt)	salare (vt)	[sa'ʎarɛ]

black pepper	pepe (m) nero	['pɛpɛ 'nɛrɔ]
red pepper	peperoncino (m)	[pɛpɛrɔn'tʃinɔ]
mustard	senape (f)	[sɛ'napɛ]
horseradish	cren (m)	['krɛn]

condiment	condimento (m)	[kɔndi'mɛntɔ]
spice	spezie (f pl)	['spɛtsiɛ]
sauce	salsa (f)	['saʎsa]
vinegar	aceto (m)	[a'tʃetɔ]

anise	anice (m)	['anitʃe]
basil	basilico (m)	[ba'zilikɔ]
cloves	chiodi (m pl) di garofano	[ki'ɔdi di ga'rɔfanɔ]
ginger	zenzero (m)	['dzɛndzɛrɔ]
coriander	coriandolo (m)	[kɔri'andɔlɔ]
cinnamon	cannella (f)	[ka'ŋɛʎa]

sesame	sesamo (m)	[sɛzamɔ]
bay leaf	alloro (m)	[al'lɔrɔ]
paprika	paprica (f)	['paprika]
caraway	cumino, comino (m)	[ku'minɔ], [kɔ'minɔ]
saffron	zafferano (m)	[dzaffe'ranɔ]

PERSONAL INFORMATION. FAMILY

58. Personal information. Forms

name, first name	**nome** (m)	['nɔmɛ]
family name	**cognome** (m)	[kɔ'ɲ'ɔmɛ]
date of birth	**data** (f) **di nascita**	['data di 'naʃita]
place of birth	**luogo** (m) **di nascita**	[ly'ɔgɔ di 'naʃita]
nationality	**nazionalità** (f)	[natsʲɔnali'ta]
place of residence	**domicilio** (m)	[dɔmi'tʃiliɔ]
country	**paese** (m)	[pa'ɛzɛ]
profession (occupation)	**professione** (f)	[prɔfɛs'sʲɔnɛ]
gender, sex	**sesso** (m)	['sɛssɔ]
height	**statura** (f)	[sta'tura]
weight	**peso** (m)	['pɛzɔ]

59. Family members. Relatives

mother	**madre** (f)	['madrɛ]
father	**padre** (m)	['padrɛ]
son	**figlio** (m)	['fiʎɔ]
daughter	**figlia** (f)	['fiʎja]
younger daughter	**figlia** (f) **minore**	['fiʎja mi'nɔrɛ]
younger son	**figlio** (m) **minore**	['fiʎɔ mi'nɔrɛ]
eldest daughter	**figlia** (f) **maggiore**	['fiʎja ma'dʒɔrɛ]
eldest son	**figlio** (m) **maggiore**	['fiʎɔ ma'dʒɔrɛ]
brother	**fratello** (m)	[fra'tɛllɔ]
sister	**sorella** (f)	[sɔ'rɛʎa]
cousin (masc.)	**cugino** (m)	[ku'dʒinɔ]
cousin (fem.)	**cugina** (f)	[ku'dʒina]
mummy	**mamma** (f)	['mamma]
dad, daddy	**papà** (m)	[pa'pa]
parents	**genitori** (m pl)	[dʒeni'tɔri]
child	**bambino** (m)	[bam'binɔ]
children	**bambini** (m pl)	[bam'bini]
grandmother	**nonna** (f)	['nɔŋa]
grandfather	**nonno** (m)	['nɔŋɔ]
grandson	**nipote** (m)	[ni'pɔtɛ]
granddaughter	**nipote** (f)	[ni'pɔtɛ]
grandchildren	**nipoti** (pl)	[ni'pɔti]
uncle	**zio** (m)	['ttsiɔ]
aunt	**zia** (f)	['ttsia]

| nephew | nipote (m) | [ni'pɔtɛ] |
| niece | nipote (f) | [ni'pɔtɛ] |

mother-in-law	suocera (f)	[su'ɔtʃera]
father-in-law	suocero (m)	[su'ɔtʃerɔ]
son-in-law	genero (m)	['dʒenɛrɔ]
stepmother	matrigna (f)	[mat'riɲa]
stepfather	patrigno (m)	[pat'riɲɔ]

infant	neonato (m)	[nɛɔ'natɔ]
baby (infant)	infante (m)	[in'fantɛ]
little boy, kid	bimbo (m)	['bimbɔ]

wife	moglie (f)	['mɔʎje]
husband	marito (m)	[ma'ritɔ]
spouse (husband)	coniuge (m)	['kɔɲjydʒe]
spouse (wife)	coniuge (f)	['kɔɲjydʒe]

married (masc.)	sposato	[spɔ'zatɔ]
married (fem.)	sposata	[spɔ'zata]
single (unmarried)	celibe	['tʃelibɛ]
bachelor	scapolo (m)	['skapɔlɔ]
divorced (masc.)	divorziato	[divɔrtsi'atɔ]
widow	vedova (f)	['vɛdɔva]
widower	vedovo (m)	['vɛdɔvɔ]

relative	parente (m)	[pa'rɛntɛ]
close relative	parente (m) stretto	[pa'rɛntɛ 'strɛttɔ]
distant relative	parente (m) lontano	[pa'rɛntɛ lɔn'tanɔ]
relatives	parenti (m pl)	[pa'rɛnti]

orphan (boy)	orfano (m)	['ɔrfanɔ]
orphan (girl)	orfana (f)	['ɔrfana]
guardian (of minor)	tutore (m)	[tu'tɔrɛ]
to adopt (a boy)	adottare (vt)	[adɔt'tarɛ]
to adopt (a girl)	adottare (vt)	[adɔt'tarɛ]

60. Friends. Colleagues

friend (masc.)	amico (m)	[a'mikɔ]
friend (fem.)	amica (f)	[a'mika]
friendship	amicizia (f)	[ami'tʃitsia]
to be friends	essere amici	['ɛssɛrɛ a'mitʃi]

pal (masc.)	amico (m)	[a'mikɔ]
pal (fem.)	amica (f)	[a'mika]
partner	partner (m)	['partnɛr]

chief (boss)	capo (m)	['kapɔ]
superior	capo (m), superiore (m)	['kapɔ], [supɛ'rɔrɛ]
subordinate	subordinato (m)	[subɔrdi'natɔ]
colleague	collega (m)	[kɔl'lega]
acquaintance (person)	conoscente (m)	[kɔnɔ'ʃɛntɛ]
fellow traveller	compagno (m) di viaggio	[kɔm'paɲɔ di wi'jadʒɔ]

classmate	**compagno** (m) **di classe**	[kɔm'paɲɔ di 'kʎassɛ]
neighbour (masc.)	**vicino** (m)	[wi'ʧinɔ]
neighbour (fem.)	**vicina** (f)	[wi'ʧina]
neighbours	**vicini** (m pl)	[wi'ʧini]

HUMAN BODY. MEDICINE

61. Head

head	testa (f)	['tɛsta]
face	viso (m)	['wizɔ]
nose	naso (m)	['nazɔ]
mouth	bocca (f)	['bɔkka]
eye	occhio (m)	['ɔkkiɔ]
eyes	occhi (m pl)	['ɔkki]
pupil	pupilla (f)	[pu'piʎa]
eyebrow	sopracciglio (m)	[sɔpra'ʧiʎɔ]
eyelash	ciglio (m)	['ʧiʎɔ]
eyelid	palpebra (f)	['paʎpɛbra]
tongue	lingua (f)	['liŋua]
tooth	dente (m)	['dɛntɛ]
lips	labbra (f pl)	['ʎabbra]
cheekbones	zigomi (m)	['ʣigomi]
gum	gengiva (f)	[ʤen'ʤiva]
palate	palato (m)	[pa'ʎatɔ]
nostrils	narici (f pl)	[na'riʧi]
chin	mento (m)	['mentɔ]
jaw	mascella (f)	[ma'ʃɛʎa]
cheek	guancia (f)	[gu'anʧa]
forehead	fronte (f)	['frɔntɛ]
temple	tempia (f)	['tɛmpia]
ear	orecchio (m)	[ɔ'rɛkkiɔ]
back of the head	nuca (f)	['nuka]
neck	collo (m)	['kɔllɔ]
throat	gola (f)	['gɔʎa]
hair	capelli (m pl)	[ka'pɛlli]
hairstyle	pettinatura (f)	[pɛttina'tura]
haircut	taglio (m)	['taʎɔ]
wig	parrucca (f)	['parrukka]
moustache	baffi (m pl)	['baffi]
beard	barba (f)	['barba]
to have (a beard, etc.)	portare (vt)	[pɔr'tarɛ]
plait	treccia (f)	['trɛʧa]
sideboards	basette (f pl)	[ba'zɛttɛ]
red-haired (adj)	rosso	['rɔssɔ]
grey (hair)	brizzolato	[britsɔ'ʎatɔ]
bald (adj)	calvo	['kaʎvɔ]
bald patch	calvizie (f)	[kaʎ'witsiɛ]

| ponytail | coda (f) di cavallo | ['kɔda di ka'vaʎɔ] |
| fringe | frangetta (f) | [fran'dʒetta] |

62. Human body

| hand | mano (f) | ['manɔ] |
| arm | braccio (m) | ['bratʃɔ] |

finger	dito (m)	['ditɔ]
thumb	pollice (m)	['pollitʃe]
little finger	mignolo (m)	[mi'ɲʲɔlɔ]
nail	unghia (f)	['ungja]

fist	pugno (m)	['puɲʲɔ]
palm	palmo (m)	['paʎmɔ]
wrist	polso (m)	['pɔʎsɔ]
forearm	avambraccio (m)	[avamb'ratʃɔ]
elbow	gomito (m)	['gɔmitɔ]
shoulder	spalla (f)	['spaʎa]

leg	gamba (f)	['gamba]
foot	pianta (f) del piede	['pjanta dɛʎ 'pjedɛ]
knee	ginocchio (m)	[dʒi'nɔkkiɔ]
calf (part of leg)	polpaccio (m)	[pɔʎ'patʃɔ]
hip	anca (f)	['aŋka]
heel	tallone (m)	[tal'lɔnɛ]

body	corpo (m)	['kɔrpɔ]
stomach	pancia (f)	['pantʃa]
chest	petto (m)	['pɛttɔ]
breast	seno (m)	['sɛnɔ]
flank	fianco (m)	['fjaŋkɔ]
back	schiena (f)	['skjena]
lower back	zona (f) lombare	['dzona lɔm'barɛ]
waist	vita (f)	['wita]

navel	ombelico (m)	[ɔmbɛ'likɔ]
buttocks	natiche (f pl)	['natikɛ]
bottom	sedere (m)	[sɛ'dɛrɛ]

beauty mark	neo (m)	['nɛɔ]
birthmark	voglia (f)	['vɔʎja]
tattoo	tatuaggio (m)	[tatu'adʒɔ]
scar	cicatrice (f)	[tʃikat'ritʃe]

63. Diseases

illness	malattia (f)	[maʎat'tia]
to be ill	essere malato	['ɛssɛrɛ ma'ʎatɔ]
health	salute (f)	[sa'lytɛ]
runny nose (coryza)	raffreddore (m)	[raffrɛd'dorɛ]
tonsillitis	tonsillite (f)	[tɔnsil'litɛ]

cold (illness)	**raffreddore** (m)	[raffrɛd'dɔrɛ]
to catch a cold	**raffreddarsi** (vr)	[raffrɛd'darsi]

bronchitis	**bronchite** (f)	[brɔ'ŋkitɛ]
pneumonia	**polmonite** (f)	[pɔlmo'nitɛ]
flu, influenza	**influenza** (f)	[infly'ɛntsa]

short-sighted (adj)	**miope**	['miɔpɛ]
long-sighted (adj)	**presbite**	['prɛzbitɛ]
squint	**strabismo** (m)	[stra'bizmɔ]
squint-eyed (adj)	**strabico**	['strabikɔ]
cataract	**cateratta** (f)	[katɛ'ratta]
glaucoma	**glaucoma** (m)	[gʎau'kɔma]

stroke	**ictus** (m) **cerebrale**	['iktus ʧeleb'ralɛ]
heart attack	**attacco** (m) **di cuore**	[at'takɔ di ku'ɔrɛ]
myocardial infarction	**infarto** (m) **miocardico**	[in'fartɔ miɔkar'dikɔ]
paralysis	**paralisi** (f)	[pa'ralizi]
to paralyse (vt)	**paralizzare** (vt)	[parali'dzarɛ]

allergy	**allergia** (f)	[aller'ʤia]
asthma	**asma** (f)	['azma]
diabetes	**diabete** (m)	[dia'bɛtɛ]

toothache	**mal** (m) **di denti**	[maʎ di 'dɛnti]
caries	**carie** (f)	['kariɛ]

diarrhoea	**diarrea** (f)	[diar'rɛa]
constipation	**stitichezza** (f)	[stiti'kɛtsa]
stomach upset	**disturbo** (m) **gastrico**	[dis'turbɔ 'gastrikɔ]
food poisoning	**intossicazione** (f) **alimentare**	[intɔsika'tsiɔnɛ alimen'tarɛ]
to have a food poisoning	**intossicarsi** (vr)	[intɔssi'karsi]

arthritis	**artrite** (f)	[art'ritɛ]
rickets	**rachitide** (f)	[ra'kitidɛ]
rheumatism	**reumatismo** (m)	[rɛuma'tizmɔ]
atherosclerosis	**aterosclerosi** (f)	[atɛrɔskle'rɔzi]

gastritis	**gastrite** (f)	[gast'ritɛ]
appendicitis	**appendicite** (f)	[appɛndi'ʧitɛ]
cholecystitis	**colecistite** (f)	[kɔleʧis'titɛ]
ulcer	**ulcera** (f)	['uʎʧera]

measles	**morbillo** (m)	[mɔr'billɔ]
German measles	**rosolia** (f)	[rɔzɔ'lia]
jaundice	**itterizia** (f)	[ittɛ'ritsia]
hepatitis	**epatite** (f)	[ɛpa'titɛ]

schizophrenia	**schizofrenia** (f)	[skidzɔfrɛ'nia]
rabies (hydrophobia)	**rabbia** (f)	['rabbja]
neurosis	**nevrosi** (f)	[nɛv'rɔzi]
concussion	**commozione** (f) **cerebrale**	[kɔmmɔ'tsiɔnɛ ʧerɛb'ralɛ]

cancer	**cancro** (m)	['kaŋkrɔ]
sclerosis	**sclerosi** (f)	[skle'rɔzi]
multiple sclerosis	**sclerosi** (f) **multipla**	[skle'rɔzi 'muʎtipʎa]

alcoholism	alcolismo (m)	[aʎkɔ'lizmɔ]
alcoholic (n)	alcolizzato (m)	[aʎkɔli'dzato]
syphilis	sifilide (f)	[si'filidɛ]
AIDS	AIDS (m)	['aids]

tumour	tumore (m)	[tu'mɔrɛ]
fever	febbre (f)	['fɛbbrɛ]
malaria	malaria (f)	[ma'ʎaria]
gangrene	cancrena (f)	[kaŋk'rɛna]
seasickness	mal (m) di mare	[maʎ di 'marɛ]
epilepsy	epilessia (f)	[ɛpiles'sia]

epidemic	epidemia (f)	[ɛpidɛ'mia]
typhus	tifo (m)	['tifɔ]
tuberculosis	tubercolosi (f)	[tuberkɔ'lɔzi]
cholera	colera (m)	[kɔ'lera]
plague (bubonic ~)	peste (f)	['pɛstɛ]

64. Symptoms. Treatments. Part 1

symptom	sintomo (m)	['sintɔmɔ]
temperature	temperatura (f)	[tɛmpɛra'tura]
fever	febbre (f) alta	['fɛbbrɛ 'aʎta]
pulse	polso (m)	['pɔʎsɔ]

giddiness	capogiro (m)	[kapɔ'dʒirɔ]
hot (adj)	caldo	['kaʎdɔ]
shivering	brivido (m)	['briwidɔ]
pale (e.g. ~ face)	pallido	['pallidɔ]

cough	tosse (f)	['tɔssɛ]
to cough (vi)	tossire (vi)	[tɔs'sirɛ]
to sneeze (vi)	starnutire (vi)	[starnu'tirɛ]
faint	svenimento (m)	[zvɛni'mɛntɔ]
to faint (vi)	svenire (vi)	[zvɛ'nirɛ]

bruise (hématome)	livido (m)	['liwidɔ]
bump (lump)	bernoccolo (m)	[ber'nɔkkɔlɔ]
to bruise oneself	farsi un livido	['farsi un 'liwidɔ]
bruise	contusione (f)	[kɔntuzi'ɔnɛ]
to get bruised	farsi male	['farsi 'male]

to limp (vi)	zoppicare (vi)	[dzɔppi'karɛ]
dislocation	slogatura (f)	[zlɔga'tura]
to dislocate (vt)	slogarsi (vr)	[zlɔ'garsi]
fracture	frattura (f)	[frat'tura]
to have a fracture	fratturarsi (vr)	[frattu'rarsi]

cut (e.g. paper ~)	taglio (m)	['taʎɔ]
to cut oneself	tagliarsi (vr)	[ta'ʎjarsi]
bleeding	emorragia (f)	[ɛmɔrra'dʒia]

| burn (injury) | scottatura (f) | [skɔtta'tura] |
| to burn oneself | scottarsi (vr) | [skɔt'tarsi] |

to prickle (vt)	pungere (vt)	['pundʒerɛ]
to prickle oneself	pungersi (vr)	['pundʒersi]
to injure (vt)	ferire (vt)	[fɛ'rirɛ]
injury	ferita (f)	[fɛ'rita]
wound	lesione (f)	[le'zjɔnɛ]
trauma	trauma (m)	['trauma]
to be delirious	delirare (vi)	[dɛli'rarɛ]
to stutter (vi)	tartagliare (vi)	[tarta'ʎjarɛ]
sunstroke	colpo (m) di sole	['koʎpɔ di 'sɔle]

65. Symptoms. Treatments. Part 2

pain	dolore (m), male (m)	[do'lɜrɛ], ['male]
splinter (in foot, etc.)	scheggia (f)	['skɛdʒa]
sweat (perspiration)	sudore (m)	[su'dɔrɛ]
to sweat (perspire)	sudare (vi)	[su'darɛ]
vomiting	vomito (m)	['vɔmitɔ]
convulsions	convulsioni (f pl)	[kɔnvul'sjoni]
pregnant (adj)	incinta	[in'ʧinta]
to be born	nascere (vi)	['naʃɛrɛ]
delivery, labour	parto (m)	['partɔ]
to labour (vi)	essere in travaglio	['ɛssɛrɛ in tra'vaʎɔ]
abortion	aborto (m)	[a'bɔrtɔ]
respiration	respirazione (f)	[rɛspira'ʦjɔnɛ]
inhalation	inspirazione (f)	[inspira'ʦjɔnɛ]
exhalation	espirazione (f)	[ɛspira'ʦjɔnɛ]
to breathe out	espirare (vi)	[ɛspi'rarɛ]
to breathe in	inspirare (vi)	[inspi'rarɛ]
disabled person	invalido (m)	[in'validɔ]
cripple	storpio (m)	['stɔrpjɔ]
drug addict	drogato (m)	[drɔ'gatɔ]
deaf (adj)	sordo	['sɔrdɔ]
dumb (adj)	muto	['mutɔ]
deaf-and-dumb (adj)	sordomuto	[sɔrdɔ'mutɔ]
mad, insane (adj)	matto	['mattɔ]
madman	matto (m)	['mattɔ]
madwoman	matta (f)	['matta]
to go insane	impazzire (vi)	[impa'ʦirɛ]
gene	gene (m)	['dʒɛnɛ]
immunity	immunità (f)	[immuni'ta]
hereditary (adj)	ereditario	[ɛrɛdi'tarjɔ]
congenital (adj)	innato	[i'ɲatɔ]
virus	virus (m)	['wirus]
microbe	microbo (m)	['mikrɔbɔ]
bacterium	batterio (m)	[bat'tɛrjɔ]
infection	infezione (f)	[infɛ'ʦjɔnɛ]

66. Symptoms. Treatments. Part 3

hospital	ospedale (m)	[ɔspɛ'dale]
patient	paziente (m)	[patsi'entɛ]
diagnosis	diagnosi (f)	[di'aɲɔzi]
cure	cura (f)	['kura]
medical treatment	battaglia (f)	[bat'taʎja]
to get treatment	curarsi (vr)	[ku'rarsi]
to treat (vt)	curare (vt)	[ku'rarɛ]
to nurse (look after)	accudire un malato	[akku'dirɛ un ma'ʎatɔ]
care	assistenza (f)	[assis'tɛntsa]
operation, surgery	operazione (f)	[ɔpɛra'tsʲɔnɛ]
to bandage (head, limb)	bendare (vt)	[bɛn'darɛ]
bandaging	fasciatura (f)	[faɕa'tura]
vaccination	vaccinazione (f)	[vatʃina'tsʲɔnɛ]
to vaccinate (vt)	vaccinare (vt)	[vatʃi'narɛ]
injection, shot	iniezione (f)	[iɲje'tsʲɔnɛ]
to give an injection	fare una puntura	['farɛ 'una pun'tura]
attack	attacco (m)	[at'takkɔ]
amputation	amputazione (f)	[amputa'tsʲɔnɛ]
to amputate (vt)	amputare (vt)	[ampu'tarɛ]
coma	coma (m)	['kɔma]
to be in a coma	essere in coma	['ɛssɛrɛ in 'kɔma]
intensive care	rianimazione (f)	[rianima'tsʲɔnɛ]
to recover (~ from flu)	guarire (vi)	[gua'rirɛ]
state (patient's ~)	stato (f)	['statɔ]
consciousness	conoscenza (f)	[kɔnɔ'ʃɛntsa]
memory (faculty)	memoria (f)	[mɛ'mɔria]
to extract (tooth)	estrarre (vt)	[ɛst'rarrɛ]
filling	otturazione (f)	[ottura'tsʲɔnɛ]
to fill (a tooth)	otturare (vt)	[ottu'rarɛ]
hypnosis	ipnosi (f)	[ip'nɔzi]
to hypnotize (vt)	ipnotizzare (vt)	[ipnoti'dzarɛ]

67. Medicine. Drugs. Accessories

medicine, drug	medicina (f)	[mɛdi'ʧina]
remedy	rimedio (m)	[ri'mɛdiɔ]
prescription	prescrizione (f)	[prɛskri'tsʲɔnɛ]
tablet, pill	compressa (f)	[kɔmp'rɛssa]
ointment	unguento (m)	[uɲu'ɛntɔ]
ampoule	fiala (f)	[fi'aʎa]
mixture	pozione (f)	[pɔ'tsʲɔnɛ]
syrup	sciroppo (m)	[ʃi'rɔppɔ]
pill	pillola (f)	['pillɜʎa]

powder	**polverina** (f)	[poʎveˈrina]
bandage	**benda** (f)	[ˈbɛnda]
cotton wool	**ovatta** (f)	[ɔˈvatta]
iodine	**iodio** (m)	[iˈɔdio]

plaster	**cerotto** (m)	[ʧeˈrɔtto]
eyedropper	**contagocce** (m)	[kɔntaˈgoʧe]
thermometer	**termometro** (m)	[tɛrˈmɔmɛtro]
syringe	**siringa** (f)	[siˈriŋa]

| wheelchair | **sedia** (f) **a rotelle** | [ˈsɛdja a rɔˈtɛllɛ] |
| crutches | **stampelle** (f pl) | [stamˈpɛlle] |

painkiller	**analgesico** (m)	[anaʎˈdʒɛziko]
laxative	**lassativo** (m)	[lassaˈtivɔ]
spirit (ethanol)	**alcol** (m)	[aʎˈkɔʎ]
medicinal herbs	**erba** (f) **officinale**	[ˈɛrba ɔffiʧiˈnale]
herbal (~ tea)	**alle erbe**	[alˈlɛrbɛ]

FLAT

68. Flat

flat	appartamento (m)	[apparta'mɛntɔ]
room	camera (f), stanza (f)	['kamɛra], ['stantsa]
bedroom	camera (f) da letto	['kamɛra da 'lettɔ]
dining room	sala (f) da pranzo	['saʎa da 'prantsɔ]
living room	salotto (m)	[sa'lɔttɔ]
study	studio (m)	['studiɔ]
entry room	ingresso (m)	[iŋ'rɛssɔ]
bathroom	bagno (m)	['baɲ'ɔ]
water closet	gabinetto (m)	[gabi'nɛttɔ]
ceiling	soffitto (m)	[sɔf'fittɔ]
floor	pavimento (m)	[pawi'mɛntɔ]
corner	angolo (m)	['aŋɔlɔ]

69. Furniture. Interior

furniture	mobili (m pl)	['mɔbili]
table	tavolo (m)	['tavɔlɔ]
chair	sedia (f)	['sɛdia]
bed	letto (m)	['lettɔ]
sofa, settee	divano (m)	[di'vanɔ]
armchair	poltrona (f)	[pɔʎt'rɔna]
bookcase	libreria (f)	[librɛ'ria]
shelf	ripiano (m)	[ri'pjanɔ]
set of shelves	scaffale (m)	[ska'fale]
wardrobe	armadio (m)	[ar'madiɔ]
coat rack	attaccapanni (m) da parete	[attakka'paɲi da pa'rɛtɛ]
coat stand	appendiabiti (m) da terra	[apendi'abiti da tɛrra]
chest of drawers	comò (m)	[kɔ'mɔ]
coffee table	tavolino (m) da salotto	[tavɔ'lina da sa'lɔttɔ]
mirror	specchio (m)	['spɛkkiɔ]
carpet	tappeto (m)	[tap'pɛtɔ]
small carpet	tappetino (m)	[tap'pɛtinɔ]
fireplace	camino (m)	[ka'minɔ]
candle	candela (f)	[kan'dɛʎa]
candlestick	candeliere (m)	[kandɛ'ʎjerɛ]
drapes	tende (f pl)	['tɛndɛ]
wallpaper	carta (f) da parati	['karta da pa'rati]

blinds (jalousie)	tende (f pl) alla veneziana	['tɛndɛ aʎa vɛnɛtsi'ana]
table lamp	lampada (f) da tavolo	['ʎampada da 'tavɔlɔ]
wall lamp	lampada (f) da parete	['ʎampada da pa'rɛtɛ]
standard lamp	lampada (f) a stelo	['ʎampada a 'stɛlɔ]
chandelier	lampadario (m)	[ʎampa'dariɔ]

leg (of chair, table)	gamba (f)	['gamba]
armrest	bracciolo (m)	['bratʃɔlɔ]
back	spalliera (f)	[spa'ʎjera]
drawer	cassetto (m)	[kas'sɛttɔ]

70. Bedding

bedclothes	biancheria (f) da letto	[biaŋke'ria da 'lɛttɔ]
pillow	cuscino (m)	[ku'ʃinɔ]
pillowslip	federa (f)	['fɛdɛra]
blanket (eiderdown)	coperta (f)	[kɔ'pɛrta]
sheet	lenzuolo (m)	[lentsu'ɔlɔ]
bedspread	copriletto (m)	[kɔpri'lettɔ]

71. Kitchen

kitchen	cucina (f)	[ku'tʃina]
gas	gas (m)	[gas]
gas cooker	fornello (m) a gas	[for'nɛllɔ a gas]
electric cooker	fornello (m) elettrico	[for'nɛllɔ ɛ'lettrikɔ]
oven	forno (m)	['fornɔ]
microwave oven	forno (m) a microonde	['fornɔ a mikrɔ'ɔndɛ]

refrigerator	frigorifero (m)	[frigɔ'rifɛrɔ]
freezer	congelatore (m)	[kɔndʒeʎa'tɔrɛ]
dishwasher	lavastoviglie (f)	[ʎavastɔ'wiʎje]

mincer	tritacarne (m)	[trita'karnɛ]
juicer	spremifrutta (m)	[sprɛmif'rutta]
toaster	tostapane (m)	[tɔsta'panɛ]
mixer	mixer (m)	['miksɛr]

coffee maker	macchina (f) da caffè	['makkina da kaf'fɛ]
coffee pot	caffettiera (f)	[kaffɛt'tiera]
coffee grinder	macinacaffè (m)	[matʃinakaf'fɛ]

kettle	bollitore (m)	[bɔlli'tɔrɛ]
teapot	teiera (f)	[tɛ'jera]
lid	coperchio (m)	[kɔ'pɛrkiɔ]
tea strainer	colino (m) da tè	[kɔ'linɔ da tɛ]

spoon	cucchiaio (m)	[kuk'kjajo]
teaspoon	cucchiaino (m) da tè	[kukkia'inɔ da 'tɛ]
tablespoon	cucchiaio (m)	[kuk'kjajo]
fork	forchetta (f)	[for'kɛtta]
knife	coltello (m)	[kɔʎ'tɛllɔ]

tableware	stoviglie (f pl)	[stɔ'wiʎje]
plate (dinner ~)	piatto (m)	['pjattɔ]
saucer	piattino (m)	[pjat'tinɔ]

shot glass	bicchiere (m) da vino	[bik'kjɛrɛ da 'winɔ]
glass (~ of water)	bicchiere (m)	[bik'kjɛrɛ]
cup	tazzina (f)	[ta'tsina]

sugar bowl	zuccheriera (f)	[dzukkɛ'rjera]
salt shaker	saliera (f)	[sa'ʎjera]
pepper shaker	pepiera (f)	[pɛpi'ɛra]
butter dish	burriera (f)	[bur'rjera]

stew pot	pentola (f)	['pɛntoʎa]
frying pan	padella (f)	[pa'dɛʎa]
ladle	mestolo (m)	['mɛstɔlɔ]
colander	colapasta (m)	[koʎa'pasta]
tray	vassoio (m)	[vas'sɔjo]

bottle	bottiglia (f)	[bɔt'tiʎja]
jar (glass)	barattolo (m) di vetro	[ba'rattɔlɔ di 'vɛtrɔ]
tin, can	latta (f), lattina (f)	['ʎatta], [lat'tina]

bottle opener	apribottiglie (m)	[apribɔt'tiʎje]
tin opener	apriscatole (m)	[apris'katɔle]
corkscrew	cavatappi (m)	[kava'tappi]
filter	filtro (m)	['fiʎtrɔ]
to filter (vt)	filtrare (vt)	[fiʎt'rarɛ]

| rubbish, refuse | spazzatura (f) | [spatsa'tura] |
| rubbish bin | pattumiera (f) | [pattu'mjera] |

72. Bathroom

bathroom	bagno (m)	['baɲʲɔ]
water	acqua (f)	['akua]
tap	rubinetto (m)	[rubi'nɛttɔ]
hot water	acqua (f) calda	['akua 'kaʎda]
cold water	acqua (f) fredda	['akua 'frɛdda]

| toothpaste | dentifricio (m) | [dɛntif'ritʃɔ] |
| to clean one's teeth | lavarsi i denti | [ʎa'varsi i 'dɛnti] |

to shave (vi)	rasarsi (vr)	[ra'zarsi]
shaving foam	schiuma (f) da barba	[ski'juma da 'barba]
razor	rasoio (m)	[ra'zɔjo]

to wash (clean)	lavare (vt)	[ʎa'varɛ]
to have a bath	fare un bagno	['farɛ un 'baɲʲɔ]
shower	doccia (f)	['dɔtʃa]
to have a shower	fare una doccia	['farɛ una 'dɔtʃa]

| bath (tub) | vasca (f) da bagno | ['vaska da 'baɲʲɔ] |
| toilet | water (m) | ['vatɛr] |

sink (washbasin)	**lavandino** (m)	[ʎavan'dinɔ]
soap	**sapone** (m)	[sa'ponɛ]
soap dish	**porta** (m) **sapone**	['pɔrta sa'ponɛ]

sponge	**spugna** (f)	['spuɲja]
shampoo	**shampoo** (m)	['ʃampɔ]
towel	**asciugamano** (m)	[aʃuga'manɔ]
bathrobe	**accappatoio** (m)	[akkappa'tɔjo]

laundry (process)	**bucato** (m)	[bu'katɔ]
washing machine	**lavatrice** (f)	[ʎavat'ritʃe]
to do the laundry	**fare il bucato**	['farɛ iʎ bu'katɔ]
washing powder	**detersivo** (m) **per il bucato**	[dɛtɛr'sivɔ pɛr iʎ bu'katɔ]

73. Household appliances

TV, telly	**televisore** (m)	[tɛlewi'zɔrɛ]
tape recorder	**registratore** (m) **a nastro**	[rɛdʒistra'tɔrɛ a 'nastrɔ]
video	**videoregistratore** (m)	[widɛɔrɛdʒistra'tɔrɛ]
radio	**radio** (f)	['radiɔ]
player (CD, MP3, etc.)	**lettore** (m)	[let'tɔrɛ]

video projector	**videoproiettore** (m)	[widɛɔprɔjet'tɔrɛ]
home cinema	**home cinema** (m)	['ɔum 'tʃinɛma]
DVD player	**lettore** (m) **DVD**	[let'tɔrɛ divu'di]
amplifier	**amplificatore** (m)	[amplifika'tɔrɛ]
video game console	**console** (f) **video giochi**	['kɔnsɔle 'widɛɔ 'dʒɔki]

video camera	**videocamera** (f)	[widɛɔ'kamɛra]
camera (photo)	**macchina** (f) **fotografica**	['makkina fotɔg'rafika]
digital camera	**fotocamera** (f) **digitale**	[fotɔ'kamɛra didʒi'tale]

vacuum cleaner	**aspirapolvere** (m)	[aspira'poʎvɛrɛ]
iron (e.g. steam ~)	**ferro** (m) **da stiro**	['fɛrrɔ da 'stirɔ]
ironing board	**asse** (f) **da stiro**	['assɛ da 'stirɔ]

telephone	**telefono** (m)	[tɛ'lefɔnɔ]
mobile phone	**telefonino** (m)	[tɛlefɔ'ninɔ]
typewriter	**macchina** (f) **da scrivere**	['makkina da 'skrivɛrɛ]
sewing machine	**macchina** (f) **da cucire**	['makkina da ku'tʃirɛ]

microphone	**microfono** (m)	[mik'rofɔnɔ]
headphones	**cuffia** (f)	['kuffia]
remote control (TV)	**telecomando** (m)	[tɛlekɔ'mandɔ]

CD, compact disc	**CD** (m)	[tʃi'di]
cassette	**cassetta** (f)	[kas'sɛtta]
vinyl record	**disco** (m)	['diskɔ]

THE EARTH. WEATHER

74. Outer space

cosmos	**cosmo** (m)	['kɔzmɔ]
space (as adj)	**cosmico, spaziale**	['kɔzmikɔ], [spatsi'ale]
outer space	**spazio** (m) **cosmico**	['spatsiɔ 'kɔzmikɔ]
world	**mondo** (m)	['mɔndɔ]
universe	**universo** (m)	[uni'vɛrsɔ]
galaxy	**galassia** (f)	[ga'ʎassia]
star	**stella** (f)	['stɛʎa]
constellation	**costellazione** (f)	[kostɛʎa'tsⁱɔnɛ]
planet	**pianeta** (m)	[pja'nɛta]
satellite	**satellite** (m)	[sa'tɛllitɛ]
meteorite	**meteorite** (m)	[mɛtɛɔ'ritɛ]
comet	**cometa** (f)	[kɔ'mɛta]
asteroid	**asteroide** (m)	[astɛ'rɔidɛ]
orbit	**orbita** (f)	['ɔrbita]
to rotate (vi)	**ruotare** (vi)	[ruɔ'tarɛ]
atmosphere	**atmosfera** (f)	[atmɔs'fɛra]
the Sun	**il Sole**	[iʎ 'sɔle]
solar system	**sistema** (m) **solare**	[sis'tɛma sɔ'ʎarɛ]
solar eclipse	**eclisse** (f) **solare**	[ɛk'lissɛ sɔ'ʎarɛ]
the Earth	**la Terra**	[ʎa 'tɛrra]
the Moon	**la Luna**	[ʎa 'lyna]
Mars	**Marte** (m)	['martɛ]
Venus	**Venere** (f)	['vɛnɛrɛ]
Jupiter	**Giove** (m)	['dʒɔvɛ]
Saturn	**Saturno** (m)	[sa'turnɔ]
Mercury	**Mercurio** (m)	[mɛr'kuriɔ]
Uranus	**Urano** (m)	[u'ranɔ]
Neptune	**Nettuno** (m)	[nɛt'tunɔ]
Pluto	**Plutone** (m)	[ply'tɔnɛ]
Milky Way	**Via** (f) **Lattea**	['wia 'ʎattɛa]
Great Bear	**Orsa** (f) **Maggiore**	['ɔrsa ma'dʒɔrɛ]
North Star	**Stella** (f) **Polare**	['stɛʎa pɔ'ʎarɛ]
Martian	**marziano** (m)	[martsi'anɔ]
extraterrestrial	**extraterrestre** (m)	[ɛkstratɛr'rɛstrɛ]
alien	**alieno** (m)	[a'ʎjenɔ]
flying saucer	**disco** (m) **volante**	['diskɔ vɔ'lantɛ]
spaceship	**nave** (f) **spaziale**	['navɛ spa'tsⁱale]

space station	stazione (f) spaziale	[sta'tsione spa'tsiale]
blast-off	lancio (m)	['ʎantʃo]
engine	motore (m)	[mɔ'tɔrɛ]
nozzle	ugello (m)	[u'dʒello]
fuel	combustibile (m)	[kɔmbus'tibile]
cockpit, flight deck	cabina (f) di pilotaggio	[ka'bina di pilɔ'tadʒiɔ]
aerial	antenna (f)	[an'tɛŋa]
porthole	oblò (m)	[ɔb'lɜ]
solar battery	batteria (f) solare	[battɛ'ria sɔ'ʎarɛ]
spacesuit	scafandro (m)	[ska'fandrɔ]
weightlessness	imponderabilità (f)	[impɔndɛrabili'ta]
oxygen	ossigeno (m)	[ɔs'sidʒenɔ]
docking (in space)	aggancio (m)	[ag'gantʃɔ]
to dock (vi, vt)	agganciarsi (vr)	[aggan'tʃarsi]
observatory	osservatorio (m)	[ɔssɛrva'toriɔ]
telescope	telescopio (m)	[tɛles'kɔpiɔ]
to observe (vt)	osservare (vt)	[ɔssɛr'varɛ]
to explore (vt)	esplorare (vt)	[ɛsplɜ'rarɛ]

75. The Earth

the Earth	la Terra	[ʎa 'tɛrra]
globe (the Earth)	globo (m) terrestre	['glɜbɔ tɛr'rɛstrɛ]
planet	pianeta (m)	[pja'nɛta]
atmosphere	atmosfera (f)	[atmɔs'fɛra]
geography	geografia (f)	[dʒeɔgra'fia]
nature	natura (f)	[na'tura]
globe (table ~)	mappamondo (m)	[mappa'mɔndɔ]
map	carta (f) geografica	['karta dʒeɔg'rafika]
atlas	atlante (m)	[at'ʎantɛ]
Europe	Europa (f)	[ɛu'rɔpa]
Asia	Asia (f)	['azia]
Africa	Africa (f)	['afrika]
Australia	Australia (f)	[aust'ralia]
America	America (f)	[a'mɛrika]
North America	America (f) del Nord	[a'mɛrika dɛʎ nɔrd]
South America	America (f) del Sud	[a'mɛrika dɛʎ sud]
Antarctica	Antartide (f)	[an'tartidɛ]
the Arctic	Artico (m)	['artikɔ]

76. Cardinal directions

north	nord (m)	[nɔrd]
to the north	a nord	[a nɔrd]

| in the north | al nord | [aʎ nɔrd] |
| northern (adj) | del nord | [dɛʎ nɔrd] |

south	sud (m)	[sud]
to the south	a sud	[a sud]
in the south	al sud	[aʎ sud]
southern (adj)	del sud	[dɛʎ sud]

west	ovest (m)	['ɔvɛst]
to the west	a ovest	[a ɔ'vɛst]
in the west	all'ovest	[aʎ 'ɔvɛst]
western (adj)	dell'ovest, occidentale	[dɛʎ 'ɔvɛst], [ɔtʃidɛn'tale]

east	est (m)	[ɛst]
to the east	a est	[a ɛst]
in the east	all'est	[aʎ 'ɛst]
eastern (adj)	dell'est, orientale	[dɛ'ʎɛst], [ɔrien'tale]

77. Sea. Ocean

sea	mare (m)	['marɛ]
ocean	oceano (m)	[ɔ'tʃeanɔ]
gulf (bay)	golfo (m)	['gɔʎfɔ]
straits	stretto (m)	['strɛttɔ]

dry land	terra (f)	['tɛrra]
continent (mainland)	continente (m)	[kɔnti'nɛntɛ]
island	isola (f)	['izɔʎa]
peninsula	penisola (f)	[pɛ'nizɔʎa]
archipelago	arcipelago (m)	[artʃi'pɛʎagɔ]

bay	baia (f)	['baja]
harbour	porto (m)	['pɔrtɔ]
lagoon	laguna (f)	[ʎa'guna]
cape	capo (m)	['kapɔ]

atoll	atollo (m)	[a'tɔllɔ]
reef	reef (m)	[ri:f]
coral	corallo (m)	[kɔ'rallɔ]
coral reef	barriera (f) corallina	[bar'rjera kɔral'lina]

deep (adj)	profondo	[prɔ'fɔndɔ]
depth (deep water)	profondità (f)	[profondi'ta]
abyss	abisso (m)	[a'bissɔ]
trench (e.g. Mariana ~)	fossa (f)	['fɔssa]

| current, stream | corrente (f) | [kɔr'rɛntɛ] |
| to surround (bathe) | circondare (vt) | [tʃirkɔn'darɛ] |

| shore | litorale (m) | [litɔ'rale] |
| coast | costa (f) | ['kɔsta] |

| high tide | alta marea (f) | ['aʎta ma'rɛa] |
| low tide | bassa marea (f) | ['bassa ma'rɛa] |

| sandbank | banco (m) di sabbia | ['banko di 'sabbia] |
| bottom | fondo (m) | ['fondo] |

wave	onda (f)	['onda]
crest (~ of a wave)	cresta (f) dell'onda	['krɛsta dɛʎ 'onda]
froth (foam)	schiuma (f)	['skjyma]

hurricane	uragano (m)	[ura'gano]
tsunami	tsunami (m)	[tsu'nami]
calm (dead ~)	bonaccia (f)	[bo'natʃa]
quiet, calm (adj)	tranquillo	[traŋku'illo]

| pole | polo (m) | ['polo] |
| polar (adj) | polare | [po'ʎarɛ] |

latitude	latitudine (f)	[ʎati'tudinɛ]
longitude	longitudine (f)	[londʒi'tudinɛ]
parallel	parallelo (m)	[paral'lelo]
equator	equatore (m)	[ɛkua'torɛ]

sky	cielo (m)	['tʃelo]
horizon	orizzonte (m)	[ori'dzontɛ]
air	aria (f)	['aria]

lighthouse	faro (m)	['faro]
to dive (vi)	tuffarsi (vr)	[tuf'farsi]
to sink (ab. boat)	affondare (vi)	[affon'darɛ]
treasures	tesori (m)	[tɛ'zori]

78. Seas & Oceans names

Atlantic Ocean	Oceano (m) Atlantico	[o'tʃeano at'ʎantiko]
Indian Ocean	Oceano (m) Indiano	[o'tʃeano indi'ano]
Pacific Ocean	Oceano (m) Pacifico	[o'tʃeano pa'tʃifiko]
Arctic Ocean	mar (m) Glaciale Artico	[mar gʎa'tʃale 'artiko]

Black Sea	mar (m) Nero	[mar 'nɛro]
Red Sea	mar (m) Rosso	[mar 'rosso]
Yellow Sea	mar (m) Giallo	[mar 'dʒallo]
White Sea	mar (m) Bianco	[mar 'bjaŋko]

Caspian Sea	mar (m) Caspio	[mar 'kaspio]
Dead Sea	mar (m) Morto	[mar 'morto]
Mediterranean Sea	mar (m) Mediterraneo	[mar mɛditɛr'ranɛo]

| Aegean Sea | mar (m) Egeo | [mar ɛ'dʒeo] |
| Adriatic Sea | mar (m) Adriatico | [mar adri'atiko] |

Arabian Sea	mar (m) Arabico	[mar a'rabiko]
Sea of Japan	mar (m) del Giappone	[mar dɛʎ dʒap'ponɛ]
Bering Sea	mare (m) di Bering	['marɛ di 'beriŋ]
South China Sea	mar (m) Cinese meridionale	[mar tʃi'nɛzɛ mɛridio'nale]
Coral Sea	mar (m) dei Coralli	[mar 'dei ko'ralli]
Tasman Sea	mar (m) di Tasmania	[mar di taz'mania]

Caribbean Sea	mar (m) dei Caraibi	[mar dɛi kara'ibi]
Barents Sea	mare (m) di Barents	['marɛ di 'barɛnts]
Kara Sea	mare (m) di Kara	['marɛ di 'kara]

North Sea	mare (m) del Nord	['marɛ dɛʎ nord]
Baltic Sea	mar (m) Baltico	[mar 'baʎtikɔ]
Norwegian Sea	mare (m) di Norvegia	['marɛ di nɔr'vɛdʒa]

79. Mountains

mountain	monte (m), montagna (f)	['mɔntɛ], [mɔn'taɲia]
mountain range	catena (f) montuosa	[ka'tɛna mɔntu'ɔza]
mountain ridge	crinale (m)	[kri'nale]

summit, top	cima (f)	['ʧima]
peak	picco (m)	['pikkɔ]
foot (of mountain)	piedi (m pl)	['pjedɛ]
slope (mountainside)	pendio (m)	[pɛn'diɔ]

volcano	vulcano (m)	[vuʎ'kanɔ]
active volcano	vulcano (m) attivo	[vuʎ'kanɔ at'tivɔ]
dormant volcano	vulcano (m) inattivo	[vuʎ'kanɔ inat'tivɔ]

eruption	eruzione (f)	[ɛru'tsʲɔnɛ]
crater	cratere (m)	[kra'tɛrɛ]
magma	magma (m)	['magma]

| lava | lava (f) | ['ʎava] |
| molten (~ lava) | fuso | ['fuzɔ] |

canyon	canyon (m)	['kɛɲʲɔn]
gorge	gola (f)	['gɔʎa]
crevice	crepaccio (m)	[krɛ'paʧɔ]

| pass, col | passo (m), valico (m) | ['passɔ], ['valikɔ] |
| plateau | altopiano (m) | [aʎtɔ'pʲanɔ] |

| cliff | falesia (f) | [fa'lezija] |
| hill | collina (f) | [kɔl'lina] |

| glacier | ghiacciaio (m) | [gja'ʧajɔ] |
| waterfall | cascata (f) | [kas'kata] |

| geyser | geyser (m) | ['gɛjzɛr] |
| lake | lago (m) | ['ʎagɔ] |

plain	pianura (f)	[pja'nura]
landscape	paesaggio (m)	[paɛ'zadʒɔ]
echo	eco (f)	['ɛkɔ]

alpinist	alpinista (m)	[aʎpi'nista]
rock climber	scalatore (m)	[skaʎa'tɔrɛ]
to conquer (in climbing)	conquistare (vt)	[kɔŋkuis'tarɛ]
climb (an easy ~)	scalata (f)	[ska'ʎata]

80. Mountains names

Alps	**Alpi** (f pl)	['aʎpi]
Mont Blanc	**Monte** (m) **Bianco**	['mɔntɛ 'bjaŋkɔ]
Pyrenees	**Pirenei** (m pl)	[pirɛ'nɛi]
Carpathians	**Carpazi** (m pl)	[kar'patsi]
Ural Mountains	**gli Urali** (m pl)	[ʎi u'rali]
Caucasus	**Caucaso** (m)	['kaukazɔ]
Elbrus	**Monte** (m) **Elbrus**	['mɔntɛ 'ɛʎbrus]
Altai	**Monti** (m pl) **Altai**	['mɔnti al'taj]
Tien Shan	**Tien Shan** (m)	[tʲɛn 'ʃan]
Pamir Mountains	**Pamir** (m)	[pa'mir]
Himalayas	**Himalaia** (m)	[ima'ʎaja]
Everest	**Everest** (m)	['ɛvɛrɛst]
Andes	**Ande** (f pl)	['andɛ]
Kilimanjaro	**Kilimangiaro** (m)	[kiliman'dʒarɔ]

81. Rivers

river	**fiume** (m)	['fjymɛ]
spring (natural source)	**fonte** (f)	['fontɛ]
riverbed	**letto** (m)	['lettɔ]
basin	**bacino** (m)	[ba'tʃinɔ]
to flow into ...	**sfociare nel ...**	[sfo'tʃarɛ nɛʎ]
tributary	**affluente** (m)	[affly'ɛntɛ]
bank (of river)	**riva** (f)	['riva]
current, stream	**corrente** (f)	[kor'rɛntɛ]
downstream (adv)	**a valle**	[a 'vallɛ]
upstream (adv)	**a monte**	[a 'mɔntɛ]
flood	**inondazione** (f)	[inɔnda'tsʲonɛ]
flooding	**piena** (f)	['pjena]
to overflow (vi)	**straripare** (vi)	[strari'parɛ]
to flood (vt)	**inondare** (vt)	[inɔn'darɛ]
shallows (shoal)	**secca** (f)	['sɛkka]
rapids	**rapida** (f)	['rapida]
dam	**diga** (f)	['diga]
canal	**canale** (m)	[ka'nale]
reservoir (artificial lake)	**bacino** (m) **di riserva**	[ba'tʃinɔ di ri'zɛrva]
sluice, lock	**chiusa** (f)	['kjyza]
water body (pond, etc.)	**bacino** (m) **idrico**	[ba'tʃinɔ 'idrikɔ]
swamp, bog	**palude** (f)	[pa'lydɛ]
marsh	**pantano** (m)	[pan'tanɔ]
whirlpool	**vortice** (m)	['vortitʃe]
stream (brook)	**ruscello** (m)	[ru'ʃellɔ]

| drinking (ab. water) | **potabile** | [po'tabile] |
| fresh (~ water) | **dolce** | ['doʌʧe] |

| ice | **ghiaccio** (m) | ['gjaʧo] |
| to ice over | **ghiacciarsi** (vr) | [gja'ʧarsi] |

82. Rivers names

| Seine | **Senna** (f) | ['sɛŋa] |
| Loire | **Loira** (f) | ['lɜira] |

Thames	**Tamigi** (m)	[ta'miʤi]
Rhine	**Reno** (m)	['rɛnɔ]
Danube	**Danubio** (m)	[da'nubiɔ]

Volga	**Volga** (m)	['vɔʌga]
Don	**Don** (m)	[dɔn]
Lena	**Lena** (f)	['lena]

Yellow River	**Fiume** (m) **Giallo**	['fjymɛ 'ʤallɔ]
Yangtze	**Fiume** (m) **Azzurro**	['fjymɛ a'dzurrɔ]
Mekong	**Mekong** (m)	[mɛ'kɔŋ]
Ganges	**Gange** (m)	['ganʤe]

Nile	**Nilo** (m)	['nilɔ]
Congo	**Congo** (m)	['kɔŋɔ]
Okavango	**Okavango**	[ɔka'vaŋɔ]
Zambezi	**Zambesi** (m)	[dzam'bɛzi]
Limpopo	**Limpopo** (m)	['limpɔpɔ]

83. Forest

| forest | **foresta** (f) | [fɔ'rɛsta] |
| forest (as adj) | **forestale** | [fɔrɛs'tale] |

thick forest	**foresta** (f) **fitta**	[fɔ'rɛsta 'fitta]
grove	**boschetto** (m)	[bɔs'kɛttɔ]
clearing	**radura** (f)	[ra'dura]

| thicket | **roveto** (m) | [rɔ'vɛtɔ] |
| scrubland | **boscaglia** (f) | [bɔs'kaʎja] |

| footpath | **sentiero** (m) | [sɛn'tˈerɔ] |
| gully | **calanco** (m) | [ka'laŋkɔ] |

tree	**albero** (m)	['aʌberɔ]
leaf	**foglia** (f)	['fɔʌja]
leaves	**fogliame** (m)	[fɔ'ʎjamɛ]

falling leaves	**caduta** (f) **delle foglie**	[ka'duta 'dɛlle 'fɔʎje]
to fall (ab. leaves)	**cadere** (vi)	[ka'dɛrɛ]
top (of the tree)	**cima** (f)	['ʧima]

branch	ramo (m), ramoscello (m)	['ramɔ], [ramɔ'ʃɛllɔ]
bough	ramo (m)	['ramɔ]
bud (on shrub, tree)	gemma (f)	['dʒɛmma]
needle (of pine tree)	ago (m)	['agɔ]
fir cone	pigna (f)	['piɲja]

hollow (in a tree)	cavità (f)	[kawi'ta]
nest	nido (m)	['nidɔ]
burrow (animal hole)	tana (f)	['tana]

trunk	tronco (m)	['trɔŋkɔ]
root	radice (f)	[ra'ditʃe]
bark	corteccia (f)	[kɔr'tɛtʃa]
moss	musco (m)	['muskɔ]

to uproot (vt)	sradicare (vt)	[zradi'karɛ]
to chop down	abbattere (vt)	[ab'battɛrɛ]
to deforest (vt)	disboscare (vt)	[dizbɔs'karɛ]
tree stump	ceppo (m)	['tʃeppɔ]

campfire	falò (m)	[fa'lɔ]
forest fire	incendio (m) boschivo	[in'tʃɛndiɔ bɔs'kivɔ]
to extinguish (vt)	spegnere (vt)	['spɛɲjɛrɛ]

forest ranger	guardia (f) forestale	[gu'ardia fɔrɛs'tale]
protection	protezione (f)	[prɔtɛ'tsʲɔnɛ]
to protect (~ nature)	proteggere (vt)	[prɔ'tɛdʒɛrɛ]
poacher	bracconiere (m)	[brakkɔ'ɲjɛrɛ]
trap (e.g. bear ~)	tagliola (f)	[ta'ʎɔʎa]

| to gather, to pick (vt) | raccogliere (vt) | [rak'kɔʎjɛrɛ] |
| to lose one's way | perdersi (vr) | ['pɛrdɛrsi] |

84. Natural resources

natural resources	risorse (f pl) naturali	[ri'sɔrsɛ natu'rali]
minerals	minerali (m pl)	[minɛ'rali]
deposits	deposito (m)	[dɛ'pɔzitɔ]
field (e.g. oilfield)	giacimento (m)	[dʒatʃi'mɛntɔ]

to mine (extract)	estrarre (vt)	[ɛst'rarrɛ]
mining (extraction)	estrazione (f)	[ɛstra'tsʲɔnɛ]
ore	minerale (m) grezzo	[minɛ'rale 'grɛdzɔ]
mine (e.g. for coal)	miniera (f)	[mi'ɲjera]
mine shaft, pit	pozzo (m) di miniera	['pɔtsɔ di mi'ɲʲɛra]
miner	minatore (m)	[mina'tɔrɛ]

| gas | gas (m) | [gas] |
| gas pipeline | gasdotto (m) | [gas'dɔttɔ] |

oil (petroleum)	petrolio (m)	[pɛt'rɔliɔ]
oil pipeline	oleodotto (m)	[ɔleɔ'dɔttɔ]
oil rig	torre (f) di estrazione	['tɔrrɛ di ɛstra'tsʲɔnɛ]
derrick	torre (f) di trivellazione	['tɔrrɛ di trivɛʎa'tsʲɔnɛ]

tanker	petroliera (f)	[pɛtroˈʎjera]
sand	sabbia (f)	[ˈsabbja]
limestone	calcare (m)	[kaʎˈkarɛ]
gravel	ghiaia (f)	[ˈgjaja]
peat	torba (f)	[ˈtɔrba]
clay	argilla (f)	[arˈdʒiʎa]
coal	carbone (m)	[karˈbɔnɛ]

iron	ferro (m)	[ˈfɛrrɔ]
gold	oro (m)	[ˈɔrɔ]
silver	argento (m)	[arˈdʒentɔ]
nickel	nichel (m)	[ˈnikɛʎ]
copper	rame (m)	[ˈramɛ]

zinc	zinco (m)	[ˈdziŋkɔ]
manganese	manganese (m)	[maɲaˈnɛzɛ]
mercury	mercurio (m)	[mɛrˈkuriɔ]
lead	piombo (m)	[ˈpjombɔ]

mineral	minerale (m)	[minɛˈrale]
crystal	cristallo (m)	[krisˈtallɔ]
marble	marmo (m)	[ˈmarmɔ]
uranium	uranio (m)	[uˈraniɔ]

85. Weather

weather	tempo (m)	[ˈtɛmpɔ]
weather forecast	previsione (f) del tempo	[prɛwiziˈɔnɛ dɛʎ ˈtɛmpɔ]
temperature	temperatura (f)	[tɛmpɛraˈtura]
thermometer	termometro (m)	[tɛrˈmɔmɛtrɔ]
barometer	barometro (m)	[baˈrɔmɛtrɔ]

humidity	umidità (f)	[umidiˈta]
heat (of summer)	caldo (m), afa (f)	[ˈkaʎdɔ], [ˈafa]
hot (torrid)	molto caldo	[ˈmɔʎtɔ ˈkaʎdɔ]
it's hot	fa molto caldo	[fa ˈmɔʎtɔ ˈkaʎdɔ]

| it's warm | fa caldo | [fa ˈkaʎdɔ] |
| warm (moderately hot) | caldo | [ˈkaʎdɔ] |

| it's cold | fa freddo | [fa ˈfrɛddɔ] |
| cold (adj) | freddo | [ˈfrɛddɔ] |

sun	sole (m)	[ˈsɔle]
to shine (vi)	splendere (vi)	[ˈsplendɛrɛ]
sunny (day)	di sole	[di ˈsɔle]
to come up (vi)	levarsi (vr)	[lɛˈvarsi]
to set (vi)	tramontare (vi)	[tramɔnˈtarɛ]

cloud	nuvola (f)	[ˈnuvɔʎa]
cloudy (adj)	nuvoloso	[nuvɔˈlɔzɔ]
rain cloud	nube (f) di pioggia	[ˈnubɛ di ˈpjɔdʒa]
somber (gloomy)	nuvoloso	[nuvɔˈlɔzɔ]
rain	pioggia (f)	[ˈpjɔdʒa]

it's raining	piove	['pjɔvɛ]
rainy (day)	piovoso	[pjo'vɔzɔ]
to drizzle (vi)	piovigginare (vi)	[pjowidʒi'narɛ]

pouring rain	pioggia (f) torrenziale	['pjɔdʒa tɔrrɛntsi'ale]
downpour	acquazzone (m)	[akua'tsɔnɛ]
heavy (e.g. ~ rain)	forte	['fɔrtɛ]
puddle	pozzanghera (f)	[pɔ'tsaŋɛra]
to get wet (in rain)	bagnarsi (vr)	[ba'ɲjarsi]

mist (fog)	foschia (f), nebbia (f)	[fɔs'kia], ['nɛbbia]
misty (adj)	nebbioso	[nɛb'bjɔzɔ]
snow	neve (f)	['nɛvɛ]
it's snowing	nevica	['nɛwika]

86. Severe weather. Natural disasters

thunderstorm	temporale (m)	[tɛmpɔ'ralе]
lightning (~ strike)	fulmine (f)	['fulʌminɛ]
to flash (vi)	lampeggiare (vi)	[ʎampe'dʒarɛ]

thunder	tuono (m)	[tu'ɔnɔ]
to thunder (vi)	tuonare (vi)	[tuɔ'narɛ]
it's thundering	tuona	[tu'ɔna]

| hail | grandine (f) | ['grandinɛ] |
| it's hailing | grandina | ['grandina] |

| to flood (vt) | inondare (vt) | [inɔn'darɛ] |
| flood | inondazione (f) | [inɔnda'tsjɔnɛ] |

earthquake	terremoto (m)	[tɛrrɛ'mɔtɔ]
tremor, quake	scossa (f)	['skɔssa]
epicentre	epicentro (m)	[ɛpi'tʃentrɔ]

| eruption | eruzione (f) | [ɛru'tsjɔnɛ] |
| lava | lava (f) | ['ʎava] |

twister	tromba (f) d'aria	['trɔmba 'daria]
tornado	tornado (m)	[tɔr'nadɔ]
typhoon	tifone (m)	[ti'fɔnɛ]

hurricane	uragano (m)	[ura'ganɔ]
storm	tempesta (f)	[tɛm'pɛsta]
tsunami	tsunami (m)	[tsu'nami]

cyclone	ciclone (m)	[tʃik'lɔnɛ]
bad weather	maltempo (m)	[maʎ'tɛmpɔ]
fire (accident)	incendio (m)	[in'tʃendiɔ]
disaster	disastro (m)	[di'zastrɔ]
meteorite	meteorite (m)	[mɛtɛɔ'ritɛ]

| avalanche | valanga (f) | [va'ʎaŋa] |
| snowslide | slavina (f) | [zla'wina] |

| blizzard | tempesta (f) di neve | [tɛm'pɛsta di 'nɛvɛ] |
| snowstorm | bufera (f) di neve | ['bufera di 'nɛvɛ] |

FAUNA

87. Mammals. Predators

predator	**predatore** (m)	[prɛda'tɔrɛ]
tiger	**tigre** (f)	['tigrɛ]
lion	**leone** (m)	[le'ɔnɛ]
wolf	**lupo** (m)	['lypɔ]
fox	**volpe** (m)	['vɔʎpɛ]
jaguar	**giaguaro** (m)	[dʒagu'arɔ]
leopard	**leopardo** (m)	[leɔ'pardɔ]
cheetah	**ghepardo** (m)	[ge'pardɔ]
black panther	**pantera** (f)	[pan'tɛra]
puma	**puma** (f)	['puma]
snow leopard	**leopardo** (m) **delle nevi**	[leɔ'pardɔ 'dɛlle 'nɛwi]
lynx	**lince** (f)	['lintʃe]
coyote	**coyote** (m)	[kɔ'jotɛ]
jackal	**sciacallo** (m)	[ʃa'kallɔ]
hyena	**iena** (f)	['jena]

88. Wild animals

animal	**animale** (m)	[ani'male]
beast (animal)	**bestia** (f)	['bɛstia]
squirrel	**scoiattolo** (m)	[skɔ'jattɔlɔ]
hedgehog	**riccio** (m)	['ritʃɔ]
hare	**lepre** (f)	['leprɛ]
rabbit	**coniglio** (m)	[kɔ'niʎɔ]
badger	**tasso** (m)	['tassɔ]
raccoon	**procione** (f)	[prɔ'tʃɔnɛ]
hamster	**criceto** (m)	[kri'tʃetɔ]
marmot	**marmotta** (f)	[mar'mɔtta]
mole	**talpa** (f)	['taʎpa]
mouse	**topo** (m)	['tɔpɔ]
rat	**ratto** (m)	['rattɔ]
bat	**pipistrello** (m)	[pipist'rɛllɔ]
ermine	**ermellino** (m)	[ɛrmɛl'linɔ]
sable	**zibellino** (m)	[dʑibɛl'linɔ]
marten	**martora** (f)	['martɔra]
weasel	**donnola** (f)	['dɔŋɔʎa]
mink	**visone** (m)	[wi'zɔnɛ]

| beaver | castoro (m) | [kas'tɔrɔ] |
| otter | lontra (f) | ['lɔntra] |

horse	cavallo (m)	[ka'vallɔ]
moose	alce (m)	['aʎtʃe]
deer	cervo (m)	['tʃervɔ]
camel	cammello (m)	[kam'mɛllɔ]

bison	bisonte (m) americano	[bi'zɔntɛ amɛri'kanɔ]
aurochs	bisonte (m) europeo	[bi'zɔntɛ eurɔ'pɛɔ]
buffalo	bufalo (m)	['bufalɔ]

zebra	zebra (f)	['dzɛbra]
antelope	antilope (f)	[an'tilɔpɛ]
roe deer	capriolo (m)	[kapri'ɔlɔ]
fallow deer	daino (m)	['dainɔ]
chamois	camoscio (m)	[ka'mɔʃɔ]
wild boar	cinghiale (m)	[tʃin'gjale]

whale	balena (f)	[ba'lena]
seal	foca (f)	['fɔka]
walrus	tricheco (m)	[tri'kɛkɔ]
fur seal	otaria (f)	[ɔ'taria]
dolphin	delfino (m)	[dɛʎ'finɔ]

bear	orso (m)	['ɔrsɔ]
polar bear	orso (m) bianco	['ɔrsɔ 'bjaŋkɔ]
panda	panda (m)	['panda]

monkey	scimmia (f)	['ʃimmʲa]
chimpanzee	scimpanzè (m)	[ʃimpan'dzɛ]
orangutan	orango (m)	[ɔ'raŋɔ]
gorilla	gorilla (m)	[gɔ'riʎa]
macaque	macaco (m)	[ma'kakɔ]
gibbon	gibbone (m)	[dʒib'bɔnɛ]

elephant	elefante (m)	[ɛle'fantɛ]
rhinoceros	rinoceronte (m)	[rinɔtʃe'rɔntɛ]
giraffe	giraffa (f)	[dʒi'raffa]
hippopotamus	ippopotamo (m)	[ippɔ'pɔtamɔ]

| kangaroo | canguro (m) | [ka'ŋurɔ] |
| koala (bear) | koala (m) | [kɔ'aʎa] |

mongoose	mangusta (f)	[ma'ŋusta]
chinchilla	cincillà (f)	[tʃintʃi'ʎa]
skunk	moffetta (f)	[mɔf'fɛtta]
porcupine	istrice (m)	['istritʃe]

89. Domestic animals

cat	gatta (f)	['gatta]
tomcat	gatto (m)	['gattɔ]
dog	cane (m)	['kanɛ]

horse	cavallo (m)	[ka'vallɔ]
stallion	stallone (m)	[stal'lɔnɛ]
mare	giumenta (f)	[dʒu'mɛnta]

cow	mucca (f)	['mukka]
bull	toro (m)	['tɔrɔ]
ox	bue (m)	['buɛ]

sheep	pecora (f)	['pɛkɔra]
ram	montone (m)	[mɔn'tɔnɛ]
goat	capra (f)	['kapra]
billy goat, he-goat	caprone (m)	[kap'rɔnɛ]

| donkey | asino (m) | ['azinɔ] |
| mule | mulo (m) | ['mulɔ] |

pig	porco (m)	['pɔrkɔ]
piglet	porcellino (m)	[pɔrʧel'linɔ]
rabbit	coniglio (m)	[kɔ'niʎɔ]

| hen (chicken) | gallina (f) | [gal'lina] |
| cock | gallo (m) | ['gallɔ] |

duck	anatra (f)	['anatra]
drake	maschio (m) dell'anatra	['maskiɔ dɛʎ 'anatra]
goose	oca (f)	['ɔka]

| stag turkey | tacchino (m) | [tak'kinɔ] |
| turkey (hen) | tacchina (f) | [tak'kina] |

domestic animals	animali (m pl) domestici	[ani'mali dɔ'mɛstiʧi]
tame (e.g. ~ hamster)	addomesticato	[addɔmɛsti'katɔ]
to tame (vt)	addomesticare (vt)	[addɔmɛsti'karɛ]
to breed (vt)	allevare (vt)	[alle'varɛ]

farm	fattoria (f)	[fattɔ'ria]
poultry	pollame (m)	[pɔ'ʎamɛ]
cattle	bestiame (m)	[bɛs'tjamɛ]
herd (cattle)	branco (m), mandria (f)	['brankɔ], ['mandria]

stable	scuderia (f)	[skudɛ'ria]
pigsty	porcile (m)	[pɔr'ʧile]
cowshed	stalla (f)	['stalla]
rabbit hutch	conigliera (f)	[kɔni'ʎjera]
hen house	pollaio (m)	[pɔ'ʎajo]

90. Birds

bird	uccello (m)	[u'ʧellɔ]
pigeon	colombo (m), piccione (m)	[kɔ'lɔmbɔ], [pi'ʧɔnɛ]
sparrow	passero (m)	['passɛrɔ]
tit	cincia (f)	['ʧinʧa]
magpie	gazza (f)	['gatsa]
raven	corvo (m)	['kɔrvɔ]

crow	cornacchia (f)	[kɔr'nakkja]
jackdaw	taccola (f)	['takkoʎa]
rook	corvo (m) comune	['kɔrvɔ kɔ'munɛ]
duck	anatra (f)	['anatra]
goose	oca (f)	['ɔka]
pheasant	fagiano (m)	[fa'ʤanɔ]
eagle	aquila (f)	['akuiʎa]
hawk	astore (m)	[as'tɔrɛ]
falcon	falco (m)	['faʎkɔ]
vulture	grifone (m)	[gri'fonɛ]
condor	condor (m)	['kondɔr]
swan	cigno (m)	['ʧiɲɔ]
crane	gru (f)	[gru]
stork	cicogna (f)	[ʧi'koɲja]
parrot	pappagallo (m)	[pappa'gallɔ]
hummingbird	colibrì (m)	[kɔlib'ri]
peacock	pavone (m)	[pa'vonɛ]
ostrich	struzzo (m)	['strutsɔ]
heron	airone (m)	[ai'ronɛ]
flamingo	fenicottero (m)	[fɛni'kottɛrɔ]
pelican	pellicano (m)	[pɛlli'kanɔ]
nightingale	usignolo (m)	[uzi'nɔlɔ]
swallow	rondine (f)	['rondinɛ]
thrush	tordo (m)	['tordɔ]
song thrush	tordo (m) sasello	['tordɔ sa'zɛllɔ]
blackbird	merlo (m)	['mɛrlɔ]
swift	rondone (m)	[ron'donɛ]
lark	allodola (f)	[al'lɔdoʎa]
quail	quaglia (f)	[ku'aʎja]
woodpecker	picchio (m)	['pikkiɔ]
cuckoo	cuculo (m)	['kukulɔ]
owl	civetta (f)	[ʧi'vɛtta]
eagle owl	gufo (m) reale	['gufɔ re'ale]
wood grouse	urogallo (m)	[uro'gallɔ]
black grouse	fagiano (m) di monte	[faʤi'anɔ di 'montɛ]
partridge	pernice (f)	[pɛr'niʧe]
starling	storno (m)	['stornɔ]
canary	canarino (m)	[kana'rinɔ]
hazel grouse	francolino (m) di monte	[frankɔ'linɔ di 'montɛ]
chaffinch	fringuello (m)	[friŋu'ɛllɔ]
bullfinch	ciuffolotto (m)	[ʧuffɔ'lɔttɔ]
seagull	gabbiano (m)	[gab'bjanɔ]
albatross	albatro (m)	['aʎbatrɔ]
penguin	pinguino (m)	[piŋu'inɔ]

91. Fish. Marine animals

bream	abramide (f)	[ab'ramidɛ]
carp	carpa (f)	['karpa]
perch	perca (f)	['pɛrka]
catfish	pesce (m) gatto	['peʃɛ 'gattɔ]
pike	luccio (m)	['lytʃɔ]
salmon	salmone (m)	[saʎ'mɔnɛ]
sturgeon	storione (m)	[stori'ɔnɛ]
herring	aringa (f)	[a'riŋa]
Atlantic salmon	salmone (m)	[saʎ'mɔnɛ]
mackerel	scombro (m)	['skɔmbrɔ]
flatfish	sogliola (f)	['sɔʎɔʎa]
zander, pike perch	lucioperca (f)	[lytʃɔ'pɛrka]
cod	merluzzo (m)	[mɛr'lytsɔ]
tuna	tonno (m)	['tɔŋɔ]
trout	trota (f)	['trota]
eel	anguilla (f)	[aŋu'iʎa]
electric ray	torpedine (f)	[tɔr'pedinɛ]
moray eel	murena (f)	[mu'rɛna]
piranha	piranha (f)	[pi'raɲʲa]
shark	squalo (m)	[sku'alɔ]
dolphin	delfino (m)	[dɛʎ'finɔ]
whale	balena (f)	[ba'lena]
crab	granchio (m)	['graŋkiɔ]
jellyfish	medusa (f)	[mɛ'duza]
octopus	polpo (m)	['pɔʎpɔ]
starfish	stella (f) marina	['stɛʎa ma'rina]
sea urchin	riccio (m) di mare	['ritʃɔ di 'marɛ]
seahorse	cavalluccio (m) marino	[kaval'lytʃɔ ma'rinɔ]
oyster	ostrica (f)	['ɔstrika]
prawn	gamberetto (m)	[gambɛ'rɛttɔ]
lobster	astice (m)	['astitʃɛ]
spiny lobster	aragosta (f)	[ara'gɔsta]

92. Amphibians. Reptiles

snake	serpente (m)	[sɛr'pɛntɛ]
venomous (snake)	velenoso	[vɛle'nɔzɔ]
viper	vipera (f)	['wipɛra]
cobra	cobra (m)	['kɔbra]
python	pitone (m)	[pi'tɔnɛ]
boa	boa (m)	['bɔa]
grass snake	biscia (f)	['biʃa]

| rattle snake | serpente (m) a sonagli | [sɛr'pɛntɛ a so'naʎi] |
| anaconda | anaconda (f) | [ana'kɔnda] |

lizard	lucertola (f)	[ly'tʃertoʎa]
iguana	iguana (f)	[igu'ana]
monitor lizard	varano (m)	[va'ranɔ]
salamander	salamandra (f)	[saʎa'mandra]
chameleon	camaleonte (m)	[kamale'ɔntɛ]
scorpion	scorpione (m)	[skɔr'pʲɔnɛ]

turtle	tartaruga (f)	[tarta'ruga]
frog	rana (f)	['rana]
toad	rospo (m)	['rɔspɔ]
crocodile	coccodrillo (m)	[kɔkkɔd'rillɔ]

93. Insects

insect	insetto (m)	[in'sɛttɔ]
butterfly	farfalla (f)	[far'faʎa]
ant	formica (f)	[fɔr'mika]
fly	mosca (f)	['mɔska]
mosquito	zanzara (f)	[dzan'dzara]
beetle	scarabeo (m)	[skara'bɛɔ]

wasp	vespa (f)	['vɛspa]
bee	ape (f)	['apɛ]
bumblebee	bombo (m)	['bɔmbɔ]
gadfly	tafano (m)	[ta'fanɔ]

| spider | ragno (m) | ['raɲʲɔ] |
| spider's web | ragnatela (f) | [raɲa'tɛʎa] |

dragonfly	libellula (f)	[li'bɛllyʎa]
grasshopper	cavalletta (f)	[kaval'letta]
moth (night butterfly)	farfalla (f) notturna	[far'faʎa nɔt'turna]

cockroach	scarafaggio (m)	[skara'fadʒɔ]
tick	zecca (f)	['tsɛkka]
flea	pulce (f)	['puʎtʃe]
midge	moscerino (m)	[mɔʃe'rinɔ]

locust	locusta (f)	[lɔ'kusta]
snail	lumaca (f)	[ly'maka]
cricket	grillo (m)	['grillɔ]
firefly	lucciola (f)	['lytʃoʎa]
ladybird	coccinella (f)	[kɔtʃi'nɛʎa]
cockchafer	maggiolino (m)	[madʒo'linɔ]

leech	sanguisuga (f)	[saɲui'zuga]
caterpillar	bruco (m)	['brukɔ]
earthworm	verme (m)	['vɛrmɛ]
larva	larva (f)	['ʎarva]

FLORA

94. Trees

tree	albero (m)	[ˈaʎbɛrɔ]
deciduous (adj)	deciduo	[dɛˈʧiduɔ]
coniferous (adj)	conifero	[kɔˈnifɛrɔ]
evergreen (adj)	sempreverde	[sɛmprɛˈvɛrdɛ]
apple tree	melo (m)	[ˈmɛlɔ]
pear tree	pero (m)	[ˈpɛrɔ]
sweet cherry tree	ciliegio (m)	[ʧiˈʎjedʒɔ]
sour cherry tree	amareno (m)	[amaˈrɛnɔ]
plum tree	prugno (m)	[ˈpruɲɔ]
birch	betulla (f)	[bɛˈtuʎa]
oak	quercia (f)	[kuˈɛrʧa]
linden tree	tiglio (m)	[ˈtiʎɔ]
aspen	pioppo (m) tremolo	[ˈpɪɔppɔ ˈtrɛmɔlɔ]
maple	acero (m)	[ˈaʧɛrɔ]
spruce	abete (m)	[aˈbɛtɛ]
pine	pino (m)	[ˈpinɔ]
larch	larice (m)	[ˈʎariʧe]
fir	abete (m) bianco	[aˈbɛtɛ ˈbjaŋkɔ]
cedar	cedro (m)	[ˈʧedrɔ]
poplar	pioppo (m)	[ˈpɪɔppɔ]
rowan	sorbo (m)	[ˈsɔrbɔ]
willow	salice (m)	[ˈsaliʧe]
alder	alno (m)	[ˈaʎnɔ]
beech	faggio (m)	[ˈfadʒɔ]
elm	olmo (m)	[ˈɔʎmɔ]
ash (tree)	frassino (m)	[ˈfrassinɔ]
chestnut	castagno (m)	[kasˈtaɲɔ]
magnolia	magnolia (f)	[maˈɲɪɔlia]
palm tree	palma (f)	[ˈpaʎma]
cypress	cipresso (m)	[ʧipˈrɛssɔ]
mangrove	mangrovia (f)	[maɲˈrɔwia]
baobab	baobab (m)	[baɔˈbab]
eucalyptus	eucalipto (m)	[ɛukaˈliptɔ]
sequoia	sequoia (f)	[sɛkuˈɔja]

95. Shrubs

bush	cespuglio (m)	[ʧesˈpuʎɔ]
shrub	arbusto (m)	[arˈbustɔ]

grapevine	vite (f)	['witɛ]
vineyard	vigneto (m)	[wi'njetɔ]
raspberry bush	lampone (m)	[ʎam'ponɛ]
redcurrant bush	ribes (m) rosso	['ribɛs 'rɔssɔ]
gooseberry bush	uva (f) spina	['uva 'spina]

acacia	acacia (f)	[a'katʃa]
barberry	crespino (m)	[krɛs'pinɔ]
jasmine	gelsomino (m)	[dʒeʎsɔ'minɔ]
juniper	ginepro (m)	[dʒi'nɛprɔ]
rosebush	roseto (m)	[rɔ'zɛtɔ]
dog rose	rosa (f) canina	['rɔza ka'nina]

96. Fruits. Berries

apple	mela (f)	['mɛʎa]
pear	pera (f)	['pɛra]
plum	prugna (f)	['pruɲja]

strawberry	fragola (f)	['fragɔʎa]
sour cherry	amarena (f)	[ama'rɛna]
sweet cherry	ciliegia (f)	[tʃi'ʎjedʒa]
grape	uva (f)	['uva]

raspberry	lampone (m)	[ʎam'ponɛ]
blackcurrant	ribes (m) nero	['ribɛs 'nɛrɔ]
redcurrant	ribes (m) rosso	['ribɛs 'rɔssɔ]
gooseberry	uva (f) spina	['uva 'spina]
cranberry	mirtillo (m) di palude	[mir'tillɔ di pa'lydɛ]

orange	arancia (f)	[a'rantʃa]
tangerine	mandarino (m)	[manda'rinɔ]
pineapple	ananas (m)	[ana'nas]
banana	banana (f)	[ba'nana]
date	dattero (m)	['dattɛrɔ]

lemon	limone (m)	[li'mɔnɛ]
apricot	albicocca (f)	[aʎbi'kɔkka]
peach	pesca (f)	['pɛska]
kiwi	kiwi (m)	['kiwi]
grapefruit	pompelmo (m)	[pɔm'pɛʎmɔ]

berry	bacca (f)	['bakka]
berries	bacche (f pl)	['bakkɛ]
cowberry	mirtillo (m) rosso	[mir'tillɔ 'rɔssɔ]
wild strawberry	fragola (f) di bosco	['fragɔʎa di 'bɔskɔ]
bilberry	mirtillo (m)	[mir'tillɔ]

97. Flowers. Plants

| flower | fiore (m) | ['fjɔrɛ] |
| bouquet (of flowers) | mazzo (m) di fiori | ['matsɔ di 'fjori] |

rose (flower)	**rosa** (f)	['rɔza]
tulip	**tulipano** (m)	[tuli'panɔ]
carnation	**garofano** (m)	[ga'rɔfanɔ]
gladiolus	**gladiolo** (m)	[gʎa'diɔlɔ]

cornflower	**fiordaliso** (m)	[fjorda'lizɔ]
bluebell	**campanella** (f)	[kampa'nɛʎa]
dandelion	**soffione** (m)	[sof'fjonɛ]
camomile	**camomilla** (f)	[kamo'miʎa]

aloe	**aloe** (m)	['alɜɛ]
cactus	**cactus** (m)	['kaktus]
rubber plant	**ficus** (m)	['fikus]

lily	**giglio** (m)	['dʒiʎɔ]
geranium	**geranio** (m)	[dʒe'raniɔ]
hyacinth	**giacinto** (m)	[dʒa'tʃintɔ]

mimosa	**mimosa** (f)	[mi'mɔza]
narcissus	**narciso** (m)	[nar'tʃizɔ]
nasturtium	**nasturzio** (m)	[nas'turtsiɔ]

orchid	**orchidea** (f)	[ɔrki'dɛa]
peony	**peonia** (f)	[pɛ'ɔnia]
violet	**viola** (f)	[wi'ɔʎa]

pansy	**viola** (f) **del pensiero**	[wi'ɔʎa dɛʎ pɛn'sjerɔ]
forget-me-not	**nontiscordardimé** (m)	[nɔntiskɔrdardi'mɛ]
daisy	**margherita** (f)	[margɛ'rita]

poppy	**papavero** (m)	[pa'pavɛrɔ]
hemp	**canapa** (f)	['kanapa]
mint	**menta** (f)	['menta]

| lily of the valley | **mughetto** (m) | [mu'gɛttɔ] |
| snowdrop | **bucaneve** (m) | [buka'nɛvɛ] |

nettle	**ortica** (f)	[ɔr'tika]
sorrel	**acetosa** (f)	[atʃe'tɔza]
water lily	**ninfea** (f)	[nin'fɛa]
fern	**felce** (f)	['fɛʎtʃe]
lichen	**lichene** (m)	[li'kɛnɛ]

tropical glasshouse	**serra** (f)	['sɛrra]
grass lawn	**prato** (m) **erboso**	['pratɔ ɛr'bɔzɔ]
flowerbed	**aiuola** (f)	[aju'ɔʎa]

plant	**pianta** (f)	['pjanta]
grass	**erba** (f)	['ɛrba]
blade of grass	**filo** (m) **d'erba**	['filɔ 'dɛrba]

leaf	**foglia** (f)	['fɔʎja]
petal	**petalo** (m)	['pɛtalɔ]
stem	**stelo** (m)	['stɛlɔ]
tuber	**tubero** (m)	['tubɛrɔ]
young plant (shoot)	**germoglio** (m)	[dʒer'mɔʎɔ]

thorn	spina (f)	['spina]
to blossom (vi)	fiorire (vi)	[fˈo'rirɛ]
to fade, to wither	appassire (vi)	[appas'sirɛ]
smell (odour)	odore (m), profumo (m)	[ɔ'dɔrɛ], [prɔ'fumɔ]
to cut (flowers)	tagliare (vt)	[ta'ʎˈarɛ]
to pick (a flower)	cogliere (vt)	['kɔʎjerɛ]

98. Cereals, grains

grain	grano (m)	['granɔ]
cereals (plants)	cereali (m pl)	[ʧerɛ'ali]
ear (of barley, etc.)	spiga (f)	['spiga]

wheat	frumento (m)	[fru'mɛntɔ]
rye	segale (f)	['sɛgale]
oats	avena (f)	[a'vɛna]
millet	miglio (m)	['miʎˈɔ]
barley	orzo (m)	['ɔrʦɔ]

maize	mais (m)	['mais]
rice	riso (m)	['rizɔ]
buckwheat	grano (m) saraceno	['granɔ sara'ʧenɔ]

pea	pisello (m)	[pi'zɛllɔ]
kidney bean	fagiolo (m)	[fa'dʒɔlɔ]
soya	soia (f)	['sɔja]
lentil	lenticchie (f pl)	[len'tikkje]
beans (broad ~)	fave (f pl)	['favɛ]

COUNTRIES OF THE WORLD

99. Countries. Part 1

Afghanistan	**Afghanistan** (m)	[afˈganistan]
Albania	**Albania** (f)	[aʎbaˈnia]
Argentina	**Argentina** (f)	[ardʒenˈtina]
Armenia	**Armenia** (f)	[arˈmɛnia]
Australia	**Australia** (f)	[austˈralia]
Austria	**Austria** (f)	[ˈaustria]
Azerbaijan	**Azerbaigian** (m)	[azɛrbajˈdʒan]
The Bahamas	**le Bahamas**	[le baˈamas]
Bangladesh	**Bangladesh** (m)	[ˈbaŋʎadɛʃ]
Belarus	**Bielorussia** (f)	[bjelɔˈrussia]
Belgium	**Belgio** (m)	[ˈbɛʎdʒɔ]
Bolivia	**Bolivia** (f)	[bɔˈliwia]
Bosnia-Herzegovina	**Bosnia-Erzegovina** (f)	[ˈbɔznia ɛrtsɛˈgɔwina]
Brazil	**Brasile** (m)	[braˈzile]
Bulgaria	**Bulgaria** (f)	[buʎgaˈria]
Cambodia	**Cambogia** (f)	[kamˈbɔdʒa]
Canada	**Canada** (m)	[ˈkanada]
Chile	**Cile** (m)	[ˈtʃile]
China	**Cina** (f)	[ˈtʃina]
Colombia	**Colombia** (f)	[kɔˈlɔmbia]
Croatia	**Croazia** (f)	[krɔˈatsia]
Cuba	**Cuba** (f)	[ˈkuba]
Cyprus	**Cipro** (m)	[ˈtʃiprɔ]
The Czech Republic	**Repubblica** (f) **Ceca**	[rɛˈpubblika ˈtʃeka]
Denmark	**Danimarca** (f)	[daniˈmarka]
Dominican Republic	**Repubblica** (f) **Dominicana**	[rɛˈpubblika dɔminiˈkana]
Ecuador	**Ecuador** (m)	[ɛkvaˈdɔr]
Egypt	**Egitto** (m)	[ɛˈdʒittɔ]
England	**Inghilterra** (f)	[iŋiʎˈtɛrra]
Estonia	**Estonia** (f)	[ɛsˈtɔnia]
Finland	**Finlandia** (f)	[finˈʎandia]
France	**Francia** (f)	[ˈfrantʃa]
French Polynesia	**Polinesia** (f) **Francese**	[pɔliˈnɛzia franˈtʃezɛ]
Georgia	**Georgia** (f)	[dʒeˈɔrdʒa]
Germany	**Germania** (f)	[dʒerˈmania]
Ghana	**Ghana** (m)	[ˈgana]
Great Britain	**Gran Bretagna** (f)	[gran brɛˈtaɲja]
Greece	**Grecia** (f)	[ˈgrɛtʃa]
Haiti	**Haiti** (m)	[aˈiti]
Hungary	**Ungheria** (f)	[uŋɛˈria]

100. Countries. Part 2

Iceland	**Islanda** (f)	[iz'ʎanda]
India	**India** (f)	['india]
Indonesia	**Indonesia** (f)	[indɔ'nɛzia]
Iran	**Iran** (m)	['iran]
Iraq	**Iraq** (m)	['irak]
Ireland	**Irlanda** (f)	[ir'ʎanda]
Israel	**Israele** (m)	[izra'ɛle]
Italy	**Italia** (f)	[i'talia]
Jamaica	**Giamaica** (f)	[dʒa'majka]
Japan	**Giappone** (m)	[dʒap'pɔnɛ]
Jordan	**Giordania** (f)	[dʒor'dania]
Kazakhstan	**Kazakistan** (m)	[ka'zakistan]
Kenya	**Kenya** (m)	['kɛnia]
Kirghizia	**Kirghizistan** (m)	[kir'gizistan]
Kuwait	**Kuwait** (m)	[ku'vɛjt]
Laos	**Laos** (m)	['ʎaɔs]
Latvia	**Lettonia** (f)	[let'tɔnia]
Lebanon	**Libano** (m)	['libanɔ]
Libya	**Libia** (f)	['libia]
Liechtenstein	**Liechtenstein** (m)	['liktɛnstajn]
Lithuania	**Lituania** (f)	[litu'ania]
Luxembourg	**Lussemburgo** (m)	[lyssɛm'burgɔ]
Macedonia	**Macedonia** (f)	[matʃe'dɔnia]
Madagascar	**Madagascar** (m)	[madagas'kar]
Malaysia	**Malesia** (f)	[ma'lezia]
Malta	**Malta** (f)	['maʎta]
Mexico	**Messico** (m)	['messikɔ]
Moldavia	**Moldavia** (f)	[mɔʎ'dawia]
Monaco	**Monaco** (m)	['mɔnakɔ]
Mongolia	**Mongolia** (f)	[mɔ'ŋolia]
Montenegro	**Montenegro** (m)	[mɔntɛ'nɛgrɔ]
Morocco	**Marocco** (m)	[ma'rɔkkɔ]
Myanmar	**Birmania** (f)	[bir'mania]
Namibia	**Namibia** (f)	[na'mibia]
Nepal	**Nepal** (m)	[nɛ'paʎ]
Netherlands	**Paesi Bassi** (m pl)	[pa'ɛzi 'bassi]
New Zealand	**Nuova Zelanda** (f)	[nu'ɔva dʒɛ'ʎanda]
North Korea	**Corea** (f) **del Nord**	[kɔ'rɛa dɛʎ nɔrd]
Norway	**Norvegia** (f)	[nɔr'vɛdʒa]

101. Countries. Part 3

Pakistan	**Pakistan** (m)	['pakistan]
Palestine	**Palestina** (f)	[pales'tina]
Panama	**Panama** (m)	['panama]
Paraguay	**Paraguay** (m)	[paragu'aj]

Peru	Perù (m)	[pɛ'ru]
Poland	Polonia (f)	[po'lɔnia]
Portugal	Portogallo (f)	[pɔrtɔ'gallɔ]
Romania	Romania (f)	[rɔma'nia]
Russia	Russia (f)	['russia]

Saudi Arabia	Arabia Saudita (f)	[a'rabia sau'dita]
Scotland	Scozia (f)	['skɔʦia]
Senegal	Senegal (m)	[sɛnɛ'gaʎ]
Serbia	Serbia (f)	['sɛrbia]
Slovakia	Slovacchia (f)	[zlɔ'vakkia]
Slovenia	Slovenia (f)	[zlɔ'vɛnia]

South Africa	Repubblica (f) Sudafricana	[rɛ'pubblika sudafri'kana]
South Korea	Corea (f) del Sud	[kɔ'rɛa dɛʎ sud]
Spain	Spagna (f)	['spaɲ'a]
Suriname	Suriname (m)	[suri'namɛ]
Sweden	Svezia (f)	['zvɛʦia]
Switzerland	Svizzera (f)	['zwiʦɛra]
Syria	Siria (f)	['siria]

Taiwan	Taiwan (m)	[taj'van]
Tajikistan	Tagikistan (m)	[ta'ʤikistan]
Tanzania	Tanzania (f)	[tan'ʣania]
Tasmania	Tasmania (f)	[taz'mania]
Thailand	Tailandia (f)	[taj'landia]
Tunisia	Tunisia (f)	[tuni'zia]
Turkey	Turchia (f)	[tur'kia]
Turkmenistan	Turkmenistan (m)	[turk'mɛnistan]

Ukraine	Ucraina (f)	[uk'raina]
United Arab Emirates	Emirati (m pl) Arabi	[ɛmi'rati 'arabi]
United States of America	Stati (m pl) Uniti d'America	['stati u'niti da'mɛrika]
Uruguay	Uruguay (m)	[urugu'aj]
Uzbekistan	Uzbekistan (m)	[uz'bɛkistan]

Vatican	Vaticano (m)	[vati'kanɔ]
Venezuela	Venezuela (f)	[vɛnɛʦu'ɛʎa]
Vietnam	Vietnam (m)	['vjetnam]
Zanzibar	Zanzibar	['ʣanʣibar]

14670799R00057

Printed in Great Britain
by Amazon.co.uk, Ltd.,
Marston Gate.